HANDS OFF NOT AN OPTION!

THE REMINISCENCE MUSEUM
MIRROR OF A HUMANISTIC CARE PHILOSOPHY

PROF. DR. HANS MARCEL BECKER
Assisted by Inez van den Dobbelsteen-Becker and Topsy Ros

Eburon
2011

TABLE OF CONTENTS

Appendix

FOREWORD

When I set out for my working visit to Humanitas – Akropolis, I had no idea I would be in for such a surprise. Where silence is usually predominant in other nursing homes, and lonely residents are either staring into space, or are dozing off, the atmosphere here was brimming with life. Music, belly dancers, happy people at the bar and a well occupied internet-café. Could one still call this a nursing home? Certainly, but one where life is lived to the full. Where life itself is at the centre; chaotic, full of fun, and adventurous. The age-proof approach in optima forma. A concept worthy of implementation in other nursing homes, without turning them into an exact copy of Humanitas, of course.

But possibly the greatest surprise was the museum. The Humanitas reminiscence museum represents a significant innovation in the elderly care, by breaking through the behavioural routines and appealing to the unique memory scope of every senior citizen. Looking at the furniture and other items of bygone days will trigger recollections and stories. It is wonderful to observe how elderly residents will recount their life-stories to others, guided by the exhibition. It certainly contributes to the well-being of the residents and provides an "extra" for visitors. Besides, it can be easily facilitated - be it on a smaller scale - by other institutions. This book will contribute to this by outlining an easy and simple way to set up such an undertaking.

I wish you, the reader, much enjoyment with the book, and Humanitas to be successful on their path to further innovation of the organization.

Jet Bussemaker

State Secretary of Health, Welfare and Sports.

MEMORIES ARE OF ALL TIMES AND GENERATIONS

One of the many aspects of loneliness is having a memory and not being able to talk about it.
Brigitte Bardot

Where the interest is lost, the memory will follow soon.
Johann Wolfgang von Goethe.
And, following him: Where the memory is activated, the interest will follow soon.
Hans Marcel Becker

The most pleasant of pleasant things is their recollection
Godfried Bomans

Through the ages, old people have always claimed that things were better when they were young, but nowadays their lives are complicated by the circumstance that they were right.
Simon Carmiggelt

Memory is like a dog lyin down at will.
Cees Nooteboom
Reminiscence museums provide nice lie-down places for the purpose (h.b.)

Brother and sister Becker discussing a painting of a destructed Rotterdam in WW II

INTRODUCTION AND ACKNOWLEDGEMENTS FOR THE ENGLISH EDITION

The reminiscence museum, its purpose and effectiveness described in this book, is not a separate item, but an integral part of the Humanitas care philosophy, modelled on humanistic principles. In order to provide clients with some measure of happiness, the elements of being in control, active participation, a positive atmosphere (yes-culture) and a sense of family-belonging are of the utmost importance. All of these elements are scoring highly in the reminiscence museum.

To those who have contributed to this book, I owe a word of gratitude. First and foremost, to my two right hands and supports in times of need, Topsy Ros and Dick Pettinga. Dick critically monitoring the work in progress and tirelessly improving it, Topsy continually introducing new literature and new perspectives. For the English version Paul van Aken and Wesley de Keyzer developed a beautiful and empathic lay-out. I also thank my secretarial staff. Likewise, I am grateful to the photographers, the scores of volunteers and the visitors who brought along their fine stories and Bert Post as a general assistant and corrector.
A special word of acknowledgement I have for the translator Francine Graafmans - Immink who translated not only with her knowledge but also with her heart.
I count myself lucky to have obtained the permission of the authors of *"Corporate Stories"* to incorporate their *Corporate Story* of Humanitas as an appendix to this book.
I would like to use this opportunity to express my gratitude to my parents (both almost 100 years old) for what they, as extended family members, with their experiential expertise, have contributed to the development of the Humanitas concept in general, and the reminiscence museum in particular. Especially, I would like to thank my sister Inez van den Dobbelsteen-Becker, volunteer/curator, who, with her fantastic detailed knowledge, has enriched this book immensely. Her unwavering participation has been extremely valuable. She knows in such a pleasing way how to commit people, especially the volunteer workers, to the cause.
Last but not least, I am extremely pleased that former Minister of Health, Pieter Winsemius, has agreed to receive the first copy of the Dutch version and the State Secretary of Health, Welfare and Sports to write the foreword.

I have endeavoured to use the reminiscence museum as leverage to portray the Humanitas care philosophy in a more playful way. This resulted also in a beautiful and instructive photobook. It has been deliberately written as some kind of manual, based on theory as well as practice,

and divided into practical compartments, in the hope that the Humanitas reminiscence museum concept will be followed up in other parts of the country and abroad.

Groups of interested initiators are hereby cordially invited to come to Rotterdam and have a look for themselves! This kind of care innovation is all about creating as much human happiness as possible, which, as an underlying purpose, is fully endorsed by Humanitas. Humanitas is a non-profit organization and has developed her expertise with community funds and private donations and does not hold corporate secrets. We do, however, hope you will not blame us for being just a little proud of what we have accomplished.

I wish you enjoyment with reading this book. Please put the knowledge you gained to good use, and pass it on. Let's open up reminiscence museums all over the world!

Rotterdam, Spring 2011

Hans Marcel Becker

In the past nursing homes tried to imitate hospitals as the white uniforms show

THE DILEMMA IN CONTEMPORARY ELDERLY CARE

THE DILEMMA IN CONTEMPORARY ELDERLY CARE

Do we spend the available funds exclusively on "care" or on "well-being" as well? After all, an euro can only be spent once.
There is an increasing awareness that the core-business of contemporary care facilities is actually creating human happiness, and the service of cure and care is only part of this. Putting it more strongly: the traditional service of cure and care has a tendency to create such negative side-effects with regards to human happiness, that it might just as well be partly abandoned. Gigerenzer mentions on the subject not to ask the doctor for his recommendations, but to ask him what he would do if it concerned his mother. Care institutions should, therefore, look at their clientele from that angle: "Would my mother feel comfortable to be regarded as a mere object of medical and paramedical treatment?" This implies that great changes on managerial level need to take place in the elderly care.
Schutte and Hendriks formulate it in this way: "Becker wanted more quality of life for the residents, a vision which would turn the entire financial structure in care-land upside-down." In fact, the "Becker-approach" to

Nursing homes of the sixties, here Humanitas-Akropolis (then named Humanitas Clinic) were unattractive, like upended matchboxes. The car park is now a park (see page 36-37)

happiness is not more expensive at all. Once living standards have been improved to an extent that clients have less to complain, become active, and family and volunteer workers are more inclined to visit, everything turns out to be cheaper. Additionally it will be easier to recruit staff, sick leave becomes less frequent, and there is less personnel fall-out.

The existing medical/therapeutic approach with its accent on hygiene and medication can be easily explained from history. It dates back to the time when the nursing home was founded as some kind of imitation hospital, as was stipulated by Dutch law over 60 years ago. This "institution" had its focus on revalidation, healing, and sending elderly "patients" home. Now that the nursing home has increasingly grown into a living arrangement for residents with non-curable chronic handicaps, the situation has changed drastically. Once established that the handicaps are incurable, the time has come to focus more on learning how to cope with those handicaps, making them fade into the background. The pre-occupation with medical and paramedical issues may have an adverse effect in such cases. Providing distractions, enjoying activities together, having something to talk about, to discuss, having something to look forward to, will turn the attention away from the problem. Distractions in the form of activities, pets and an animal farm, "eat, drink and be merry", the hairdresser's and beauty salon, meditation, spiritual guidance, or simply giving attention, can all be provided. Getting together, reminiscing - which is largely what the reminiscence museum is about – is an excellent way to forget about old-age handicaps.
An important aspect of obtaining human happiness is found in the struggle against loneliness and isolation. With the extension of the average maximum age, the decrease in offspring, a growing multi ethnical society, and an increased mobility, the chance on spending the last decades of one's life in solitude, multiplies accordingly. It is possible with a certain desperate determination, combined with a degree of creativity and with the help of modern high-tech facilities, that one might actually beat the odds. But not everyone has either the determination, or the energy to do so. Which could lead to depression. Medication or paramedical treatment will then only have a limited effect. Therefore depression, in the elderly between 65 and 80 years of age – the category populating the care centres - is regarded one of the more common ailments. More than twenty percent of elderly home residents are diagnosed with symptoms of depression. Symptoms which are quite easily mistaken for dementia, forgetfulness, confusion, a tendency to complain, somatic symptoms, grief, or loneliness, all of which have their influence on the rather flattering percentage. Loneliness and depression being hard to conquer with medication alone,

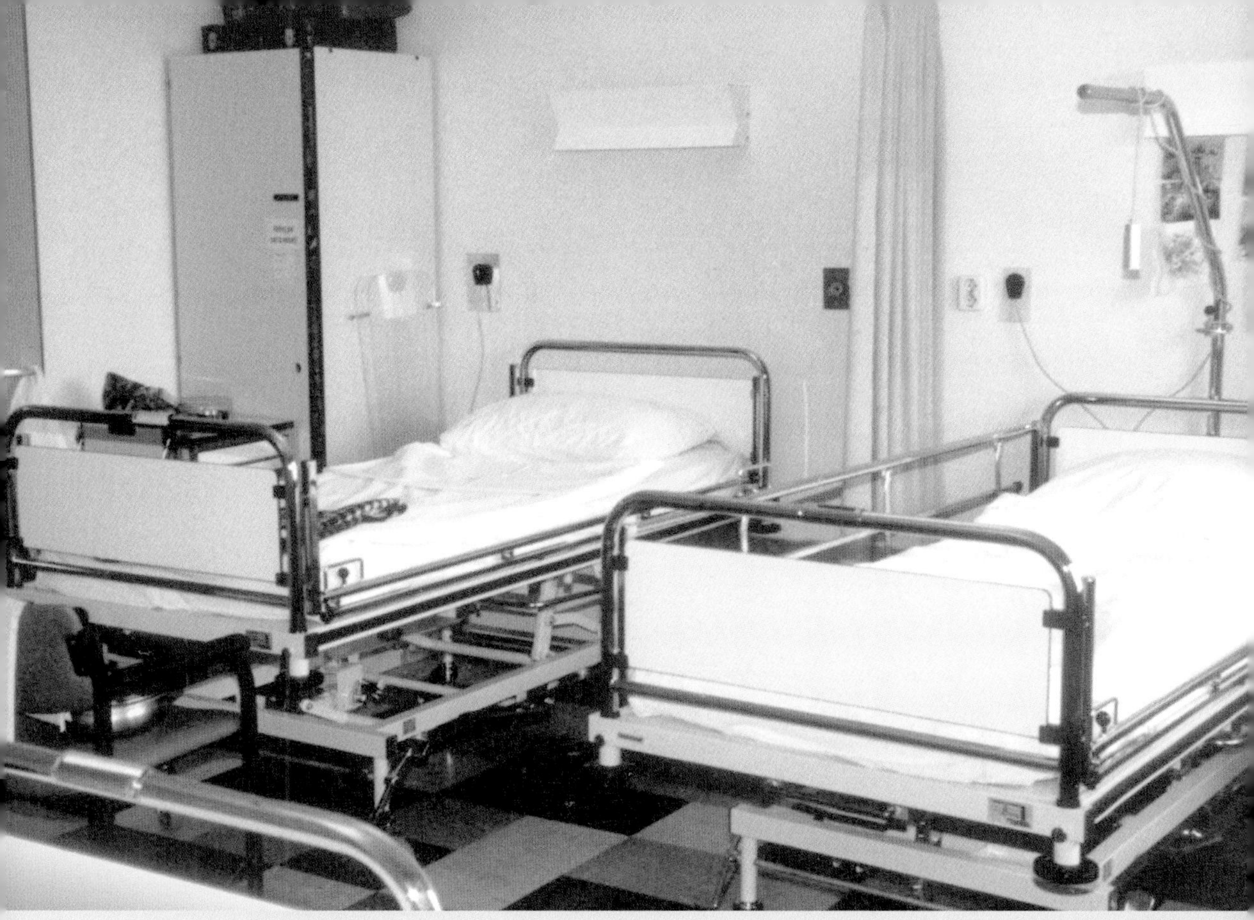

The equipment was hospital-like and clients were treated like 'patients'

other means need to be added in order to achieve human happiness. With clients whose abilities like mobility, taste, smell, eyesight and hearing are impaired, it is imperative to explore what is still possible, find the means to activate them, create excitement, and provide a group identity. These undertakings need not necessarily involve the client directly, but might be passed on by others. If, for instance, the family is offered a pleasant diversion to look forward to, this will reflect directly and positively on the client. Visits from, and the close ties with, someone's relatives are usually regarded as extremely important to the clients, who will experience this as a great enhancement of their happiness.

This could, naturally, be projected on an "extended family". We are a species who like company, and feel at home in a group. Not necessarily our own family group, but a group nonetheless, for instance a group of volunteer workers running the museum and being responsible for it. Creating a group sense is, therefore, also one of the means / assignments for the contemporary care organization.

It is my intention with this book, based on my years of practice at

Humanitas and my theoretical insight, to illuminate how the reminiscence museum could be an effectual tool for this purpose.
The way to effectuate this, by using a great variety of objects, is to trigger the mind into remembering the personal past (reminiscence) and to share these autobiographic memories with others, collectively. It causes new social relationships to be explored, nurtured and consolidated. Collective reminiscence is also used to re-interpret one's own past in order to look back on it with a degree of satisfaction, and for unsolved issues or conflicts to be processed as yet. The museum provides meeting places, "lieux de mémoires" ("places of memories") for those participating in the shared memory. It will nourish the flow of ideas and views of the collective, the group. The reminiscence museum, therefore, as are many other regional museums, is what may be called a real community museum, carried and nourished by the group of people working and living in its surroundings. Still, the reminiscence museum is clearly meant to serve beyond the target-group. There is no intention of excluding any persons or groups, on the contrary, the low threshold, and open use of immaterial testimonies and the collective memory, will ensure enjoyment for everyone, enhanced by the welcoming presentation of the objects on exhibit.

Mr Jansen, already 25 years a Humanitas client of is very pleased with the new innovation of reminiscence museums. His family is visiting him more frequently and he can tell all his stories from the past

The most pleasant of pleasant things is their recollection

Het meest gespeelde spel
Mens
erger je niet!

Chapter 2

The importance of creating a social network

THE IMPORTANCE OF CREATING A SOCIAL NETWORK

When people of one's age group, like partners, friends, cousins, old school comrades, neighbours and ex-colleagues, have disappeared from one's life, and one is prey to loneliness, it is difficult for the single individual to find a way out of this by, for instance, making it his business to create a new social network. The care organization has a history of providing a variety of means to eliminate loneliness, such as activity coaching, communal celebrations of the festive season with Christmas and New Year, Halloween and having occasional outings to, for instance football matches. Daily provisions are made in drinking coffee together, sharing meals, having a drink at the bar, playing bingo, and celebrating birthdays.

However, it is so important to realize that even within a large group of people it is possible to feel utterly lonely. Often it will not suffice for the care organization to offer external activities, pets, or human company. It needs to be catchy, and create receptivity. Somehow, it should strike a chord inside. And the reminiscence museum finds ways to strike that chord over and over.

Somehow, it should strike a chord on the inside

Examples of "conversation pieces" to (re)create the feeling of belonging to a group, and fun, as in the case of the "nails-sculpture" depicting Managing Director Hans Becker (made by one of the client/volunteers)

A Dutch television documentary once portrayed elderly people trying to survive in an anonymous society, filled with high-tech gadgets, and showed the subsequent negative side-effects from the perspective of loneliness. This Brave New World approach is, therefore, a far cry from the simple human happiness and social interaction, as offered by the reminiscence museum.

With the disappearance of the traditional introvert care- and nursing homes, where residents, robbed of their income, pets, and own home, were " just staying" and be looked after in kind, the happy community feeling as a by-product of these classical institutions has also disappeared. This certainly is a responsibility to be picked up by contemporary care institutions, where a great deal of the work is done in apartments, either rented or purchased by the clients themselves, which, however stimulating for their self-control and self-esteem, will also increase the risk of isolation. Social networking and providing "conversation pieces" are ways to rekindle the sense of belonging and happiness. The big question is, how to activate people and tease them into excitement. In my book "The Art of Living in Later Life" I have made an endeavour to contribute to this question.

One of the possibilities, it appears, is "social sharing", the sharing of collective memories, emotions, traumas. Also, sharing anecdotes between former colleagues will enhance the feeling of belonging. The difference between memories shared, and

those which are not, is considerable when talking about emotional events. The influence of "social sharing" when processing emotional events on a cognitive and social level is, according to J.K. Scherpen if I interpret him correctly, due to three factors, firstly a large-scale, multi disciplinary search for the meaning, follows by a collective endeavour to make sense of what really happened, after which followed a collective attempt to bring a new order to what took place in the past. In other words: a consciously created interactive process emerges, which helps to reduce one's sense of loneliness.

Another possibility to reduce the existing loneliness within the contemporary care institutions is the creation of a kind of substitute family. The

If the restaurants for the elderly are attracting external clientele which, in turn, is so important for the wellbeing of the residents, they should be "real" quality restaurants with a matching menu and ambiance

aim of such an "extended family" is to bring back a feeling of belonging. Within the case of Humanitas we speak of the Humanitas-family. Not only the clients and staff, but also their partners, the rest of the real family, the volunteer workers, and even the suppliers and cleaning staff are part of it; the so-called "stake-holders". The possibility of social sharing does not actually end there. The attention could also be focused on the outside world. When visitors are drawn in from outside due to provision of a real restaurant (in other words, not some sterile, lifeless, old-age canteen serving the daily grub on Formica tables and ditto standardized chairs, with uninspired staff), they will also use the cosy bar and the internet-café, thus providing topics of conversation for the clients. This will certainly be good

for their well-being. A client's happiness is sometimes better served by providing distractions for the family, rather than for the client directly. When the family comes to visit, the client, with or without professional care, will be happy at any rate. Having a bar, restaurant, internetcorner and a small supermarket to service the neighbourhood as well, will give both visitors and senior residents something to talk about and to make contact. When a provision is made by providing space, ambiance, snacks and drinks, to accommodate the neighbourhood bridge-club, this will bring liveliness and entertainment. Which is why the beauty salon, the hairdresser's, the pedicure and physiotherapist should also draw clients from "the outside". As should the laundrettes, the cash points and the nurseries. Anything to break through the monotony of the day, by being in contact with the "outside world", is welcome.

It is all about liveliness and entertainment. Which is why the bar, restaurant and supermarket, as well as the beauty salon, hairdresser's, pedicure's and physiotherapist should also cater for the "outside". All this in a strictly non-medical ambiance, as shown here in the physiotherapy room, decorated as an aquarium with a variety of fish, crab, sea-horses and even a real-life deep sea diver

"Belonging to a group" implies being involved in communication. Anything contributing to that effect is of great importance to disabled clients who, in the absence of family, work or sports, would otherwise be deprived of topics of conversation.

One of the possibilities a care organization might consider for providing conversation pieces is the use of objects. All kinds of objects will do, but especially those objects with a link to emotions and past events will fit the bill. A painting of a nude, or an (imitation) abstract by Mondriaan are quite different things. Real-life pets which can bite you, or pee in a corner, provide other conversation topics than a stuffed animal, or sculpture. Which is why paintings and murals (perfect for decorating entrance halls, as they are hard to steal), sculptures and parrots and other pets are a definite "must".

Activity and self-empowerment -use it or lose it- are very important in creating happiness

As are luxurious interior decorations and furnishings with plants, aquariums and fine chandeliers. Something initially regarded as maybe an extravagant luxury (and therefore not financed by a thrifty government, solely focussed on the cure and care business), is in fact not a luxury in the elderly care. The animal farm, the sculpture gardens, the Koi carp ponds, they all belong to the same category. In this way Humanitas Rotterdam has been able to enrich their communal areas with two sculpture gardens, which together hold more than 60 bronze sculptures and relief art. As long as it offers something to talk about, be it good, or bad. A pony drowning in a pond measures up to the criteria of conversation pieces, as much as a pony giving birth to her endearing fowl.

All of the abovementioned stimuli will cause people from outside to come and visit the care centres, if only to have a bite to eat, or go to the hairdresser's. Visitors are superb conversation pieces. There is nothing more fun than to talk and gossip about other people. ("Oh, I say, my dear, have a look at the sight of that woman over there, thinking she can get away with purple hair at her age, it just won't do, is what I say.."). There is an increasing awareness of gossip having an underlying, deeper implication. Gossip researchers are associating the act of gossiping with the acquirement, loss, or preservation of power. Gossiping might, therefore, be considered an expression of reputation management, as is frequently observed in care homes. Gossiping ought not to be judged too harshly, and the same goes for complaining (for some clients the saying goes: "a day without complaints, is a day not lived").

A rather specific category of conversation pieces is provided by the household objects from bygone days. All those tools and utensils used at work or at home for decades, have had a tremendous influence on our lives. Those are the objects, together with photographs, paintings, smells and sounds, one might encounter again in the reminiscence museum, sometimes even half a century later. These are also the objects which help recall the autobiographical memories. The kind of reminiscence is multi-functional not only on a personal level (processing the past, and giving direction to the future), but on a cognitive level as well (preventing a loss of mental abilities), but in particular on a social level.

Real-life animals who can bark or wag their tail, and pee, will do more to stimulate a conversation than any sculpture will, however beautiful it might be

Parks instead of parking places!

Being able to recount one's memories on seeing the objects will provide social interaction, and a connection with other people. It is an integration of the many aspects of these household objects, including their sound, smell, and touchy-feely quality. Add to this the process of shared recollection and exchange of memories, like how the laundry was done with a washboard and washtub, and how one fabricated beautiful artifacts on the old Singer sewing machine, to complete the picture.

These everyday household objects of the past are the core of the reminiscence museum. How the museum is operated, the reactions it evokes, which social connections are made, or strengthened, are the subjects of this study which is also based on practical experience. It will be made evident that the reminiscence museum not only stimulates the senses of sight and speech, but also those of touch, smell and hearing. This spontaneous process of enticing others to engage in shared reminiscence has proved to be a useful, and welcome innovation in the elderly care.

The effect of a painting of a nude is quite different from that of an abstract Mondriaan

Chapter 3

The reminiscence museum and "reminiscing"

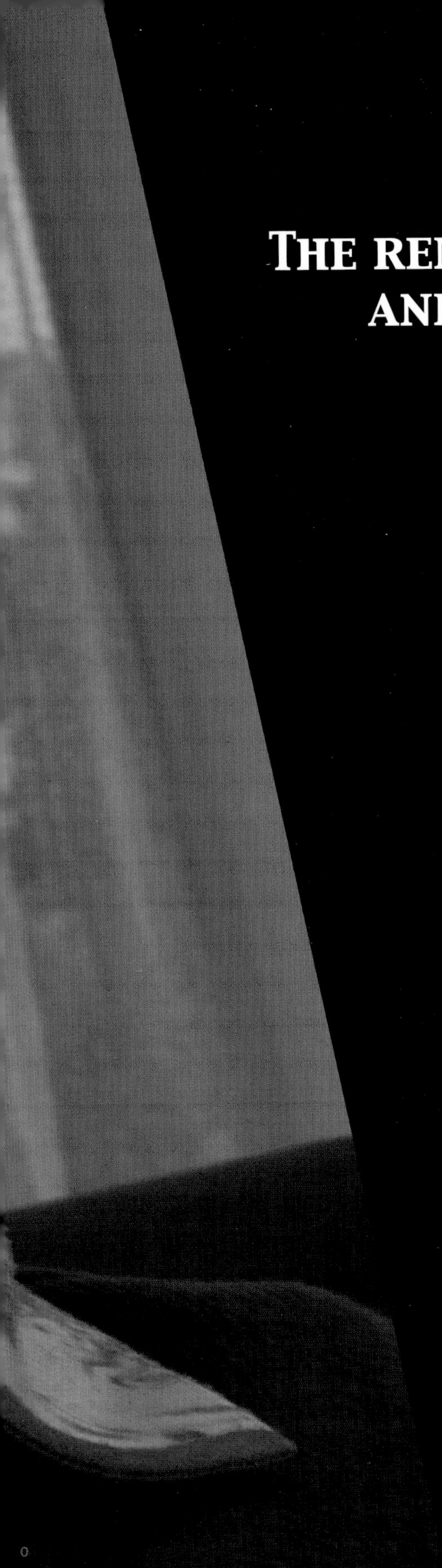

THE REMINISCENCE MUSEUM AND "REMINISCING"

The reminiscence museum collects everyday household objects from bygone days, puts them on display according their theme, provides matching illustrations, sounds and smells, and puts them totally unrestricted, literally and figuratively speaking, in the hands of the visitors.
It has been a longstanding practice in the elderly care to use household objects from the past for therapeutic purposes. The so-called "reminiscence method" is frequently practiced with for instance Alzheimer's patients. The therapist, or reminiscence worker, whilst talking about the objects on display, allowing them to be touched and handled, sometimes accompanied by their matching sounds and smells, will try to awaken memories and thereby activate the client. The term "reminiscence method", a consciously avoided phrase at Humanitas because of its medical / therapeutic connotation, creates an image of elderly people in dotage who are coaxed to recount their memories, guided by household objects from the past.
J. van Pruysenbroeck poses in his dissertation that, originally, the term reminiscence was used merely to specify the spontaneous process of remem-

Therapists used to revive their client's memories by using the "activity reminiscence" method. Nowadays, a visit to the museum will have the same effect in a much more spontaneous manner

Granddad knowing his way about the museum's tool-shed and explaining its contents to his grandson, might result in a sudden revival of a twinkle in his eyes

bering, but in the elderly care it developed an extra dimension of 'activity': the conscious stimulation of the process of remembering. This kind of 'activity' may , for instance, involve reviewing the step-by-step account of all phases of the elderly client's life.

An outstanding account of the non-conformity of memories is found in the Dutch Health Care Board's "Memories, a Matter of Dispute". What surfaces as a memory, is not just defined by what has been stored in the mind during the event. It is also the total outcome of the interaction with other memories, of signature points with the present situation, of interaction with today's stories, as is happening in the museum. Memories may be imaginary, or even induced by others. A matter of small consequence for the social interaction and happiness of the visitors to the museum. Any memory is likely to be experienced as a trustworthy and authentic representation of events from the past. However, the anomaly may be considerable. Halbwachs states, therefore, that memories are not "congealed". New representations, facts and insights will continually alter the memories. As we are always participants of new groups (for instance museum visitors), our memories will not only renew themselves, but recounting these memories within the groups appears to play an important part in the activation of

The objects are partly displayed as a theme, as in this example of a 1940 kitchen

inter-human relationships. By utilizing collective thought currents, people are quite able to define, and relate their memories but, moreover, will be able to actively get to work with them. This should not be a personal, but rather an inter-personal process. For the sake of the client, the care institution is obliged to facilitate this inter-personal process. The reminiscence museum is an important tool to accomplish this. Using the same objects as with the "classical" reminiscence method, but in a more multi-sensory and specialized display, focussing more on creating interest, and happiness. The thus activated mind, combined with the interaction of recounting memories in a group-spirited ambiance, will create awareness and liveliness. This way the shared feeling will be enhanced and the pleasure of the memories intensified. Nothing generates more pleasurable, lively and intense dialogues than objects, smells, sounds and photographs of bygone days. The yes-culture approach of Humanitas (see appendices), combined with communication by story-telling and dialogues (see Schutte en Hendriks in "Corporate Stories") could be linked up seamlessly to the abovementioned operation of the reminiscence museum.
The humanistic core values Humanitas lives by, are the fundamental equa-

lity of one's fellow conversation partners, whilst allowing consideration for any differences in social background and education. Logically, this vision precludes the museums to be set up primarily for the purpose of brain-training in a controlled setting: not for the psycho-geriatric residents, nor the somatically disabled, and certainly not for the "healthy" elderly. It is beyond question, however, that what is called brain-training in the United States, is by rights an aspect of the ensuing result of the reminiscence museums. Tom-Jan Meeuws, a columnist for one of the leading Dutch newspapers, writes: "There is no longer a controversy about the hypo-campus, the part of the brain where the memory is lodged, being improved upon by training. However, the suggestion that this could lead to a 'rejuvenation' of the brain, as most manufacturers will have us believe, and even resulting in the prevention of dementia, is doubtful, to say the least". This may be so. But what does in fact happen in the reminiscence museum, is that life is being made more joyous and lively. And, with the objective in mind to decrease loneliness and depression, it is certainly a prerequisite. Looking at the reminiscence museums in terms of brain-training, it appears that the way in which Humanitas is launching her museums as an opportunity to stimulate the brain (memory), is rather unique. The striking significance here is that the focus is on having fun, and communication (memory-sha-

The display shows everyday objects commonly known to every household during the last century. The runner beans cutter for instance with one, two or even three slicing gaps

ring), rather than on brain-fitness, as propagated in the United States. Rather than playing a Nintendo video game all by yourself in order to stimulate your brain, the reminiscence museums are facilitating a joint way of sharing memories of events and household objects long forgotten, with your own age-group, your children and grandchildren. Rejuvenation of the brain is not a major concern. However, building new relationships, or acquiring a greater appreciation for the elderly resulting from collective memories or experiences, definitely is. The fact that granddad knows his way around the tool-shed and demonstrates this to his grandson may result in a quickening of his step, a slight straightening of the back and an unmistakable twinkle in his eyes. Thus, the visit to the reminiscence museum has caused a positive emotion, which reflects considerably on the feeling of "being still in the game", of self-esteem, and the subsequent feeling of human happiness.

Therefore, displaying the household objects of the past in the right manner, with the pleasure of recognition and creating human happiness in mind, is the ultimate goal of Humanitas. Wagenaar defines the museum in general as "a place where memories are stored". An accurate description for the reminiscence museum, where memory-inducing objects are collected and displayed. When, during the process of memory-sharing, other ears are available for listening, and there are other voices to respond, affirm, or supplement, the effect could be intensified in more ways than one. The reminiscence museum is instrumental in creating a bond between clients, in strengthening the relationship between clients, staff, and volunteers, and in re-affirming the ties between relatives.

The objects on display mainly concern the everyday household objects from the last century. Some of them are displayed thematically: the living-room from the sixties, or the 1930 kitchen. Others are displayed without a particular theme but are a compilation of as many similar objects as possible: twenty biscuit tins, fifteen electric heaters or petrol stoves in a row. The selection of the latter form of display is made in the hope that people will recognize their very own biscuit tin, or heater, which will conjure up the corresponding personal memories and bring forth a conversation. We are, therefore, talking about objects commonly known to any household in the past: the runner beans cutter, with one, two, or even three gaps, the cast-iron flat iron, the old Singer sewing machine, the zinc pail and wooden wash tub. The corresponding sounds also play a special role in triggering memories: the clanging of milk-bottles in the bottle container, the specific sound of the rattle to announce the arrival of the garbage man in olden days, the sound of grinding beans in the old-fashioned coffee-mill,

Making the old gas lighter spark again will kindle some memories of the past

and the low spinning sound of the sewing machine. They are all powerful resources for triggering memories and have the potential to bring forth a conversation. Smells and scents, too, may have a significant impact. The petrol-like smell in the bicycle shed, the smell of soapy suds in the laundry room, the distinct smell of cod-liver oil, of towels put out to dry on the towel-horse by the stove, the smell of carbide from the bicycle lamp, they can all have a great impact on the perception of happiness in the elderly. Olfactory perception may – even when this faculty has decreased with age – be a more direct way of triggering memories, than the auditory, or visual perception. Needless to say that a multi-sensory experience will only enhance the intensity of the memory. Douwe Draaisma in his book "Why life seems to go faster as you grow older" elaborates on the different aspects of mind and memory. When describing the importance of visual, auditory, olfactory, gustatory and tactile stimuli, he argues that "the autobiographical memory is our most intimate companion. We grow up together. It behaves differently when we are five years old, from when we are fifteen, or sixty, even though the changes happen so gradually, that we hardly perceive them". The sensory perceptions of sight, hearing, smell and taste are,

therefore, of the utmost importance. He refers to Marcel Proust who, in this study "A la recherche du temps perdu" ("In search of lost times") describes memories of smell and taste, awakened when tasting a "*Petite Madeleine*" (a sweet breakfast bun) and a cup of lime blossom tea. Which is why in memory-psychology the effect of sensory stimuli on the recall of autobiographical memories is known as the Proust phenomenon. We have had a similar experience in the reminiscence museum. One visitor, by the scent of a near empty bottle of "Soir de Paris" perfume, was able to remember many stories about her mother. Needless to say that the reminiscence museum will have to provide a variety of scents and smells for the purpose. It is extraordinary that smells and scents in particular are having such a profound effect on the stimulation of autobiographical memories in the elderly, as the faculty for smell decreases over the years. Quite possibly, the cause may be found in the fact that memories of smells and scents from the past are not contaminated by contesting smelling experiences of the present.
Draaisma formulated this outstandingly: "Some objects, smells and tastes have simply disappeared from our society. The way some striking motor cars have imperceptibly disappeared from the scene and you stop thinking about them until one day you see one driving past again, by

Table loads of objects, some of them heart rending, such as an (intentionally) un-used Star of David from the Second World War, are being delivered at the museum

which time it is called vintage (like the old-timer "Volkswagen Beetle with spectacles"), in the same way certain smells and tastes can disappear from your life, sometimes temporarily, sometimes forever. It happens with typical toddler's food, like the wholemeal biscuit puréed with a banana and orange juice, but also with your childhood meals and dishes, which you probably ate at your parental home every week, and then never again. You either left home, or the cooking style changed, or new ranges of puddings are crowding out the more traditional ones. With the appearance of factory-produced dairy puddings, the familiar smells and tastes of home-made classics like porridge, or treacle pudding disappeared. And if, by some miraculous coincidence, we are able to taste that particular taste, or smell that particular smell again in later life, the familiar associations are still intact and lead us back effortlessly to our early memories". That "miraculous coincidence" is neither miraculous, nor a coincidence at the reminiscence museum, but a conscious campaign by the care organization to use this medium to enhance their clients' happiness.

With regard to the differences in effect on clients who are suffering from Alzheimer's, and those who are not, Draaisma comments as follows: "In an experiment by Fromhold and Larsen, thirty healthy and thirty Alzheimer's patients, all between 71 and 89 years old, were asked to spend fifteen minutes reminiscing about events which had impacted their lives. The Alzheimer's patients recorded fewer memories than the healthy group (eight against eighteen), but the division over the timeline of life did not deviate from the healthy group: most stories of the Alzheimer's patients, too, were about their adolescent years". And it is precisely this period in time which is extensively targeted by the reminiscence museum for everyone including the grandchildren.

The fact that the objects on display in the reminiscence museum may be touched and handled is cause for an additional element of pleasure and adventure. Imagine being able to try grinding the beans in the old-fashioned coffee mill again after thirty years, have a go at a cherry pip remover, pound away at the laundry in the wash tub after half a century. This is great fun. Balance yourself once more on an old Vespa scooter, or a vintage motorbike, use the insecticide hand pump with which our Dutch nation almost poisoned itself, and use the stove blackener again. Light the butane gas with a flint lighter, make the cash register ring and try your fingers on the old typewriter once more. It is all rather exiting and evokes a variety of emotions and, thus, conversation pieces, which is why: "Hands off not an option!". This scenario comes with a special bonus-feature, the activation of ties between relatives, the real family. Where, as a rule, visits from relatives are often obligatory, their attention for the never-ending complaints about ailments rather perfunctory, and are biding their time until they can leave with any

decency after ninety minutes, having a reminiscence museum at hand will give a different scenario. The museum provides the possibility for multi-generational interaction: great-grandmother reminiscing about her youth in the nineteen twenties, grandmother remembering eating sugar beets during the occupation of the second world war, mother admiring the orange gas heater from her student days in the seventies and the (great)grandchildren are looking in amazement at the old "baco" telephones and wonder how they were operated. The dial is unfamiliar to them and they do not know the background of the words "sorry, dialled the wrong number", or "wrongly connected". Even the first computers and mobile phones to them seem pre-historic. And all of them are browsing through their respective childhood books. The sense of family belonging increases, as does their inclination to revisit the care home – Humanitas in this case – and the

Regency Room, reminiscence museum
Humanitas-Bergweg (home care)

collective happiness, the core business of the care organization, will soar, if only for a short while. The clients are no longer those age-old, pathetic people leading a vegetative existence in the waiting room of death, but turn into real-life experts, with all the feelings of self-esteem and decorum into the bargain. Their pride in showing off their own museum is considerable and their willingness to contribute to it in terms of manpower or donations of objects is remarkable. Tens of cubic metres of objects, varying from old radios from the twenties, memorabilia from the war, and orange hairdryers from the seventies are lugged into the museum. Amongst them very valuable and incidentally very moving objects, such as a non-used Star of David from the Second World War (the aged owner of which, by not sewing it on to her coat, had survived the war but as she felt the end of her days approaching, brought the star along: "I thought I would bring it here, so the memory will not be lost"), the coal heater with which one tried to survive the Second World War hunger winter, and wooden splints from the First World War. Having a birthday lunch with grandfather in the restaurant and afterwards a visit to the reminiscence museum with the whole family has become a regular phenomenon at Humanitas: no dirty dishes and no grandchildren being bored and annoying after fifteen minutes. Another aspect to the reminiscence museum worth mentioning is the impact it has on the elderly volunteer worker, which will be discussed in a separate chapter. Many writers have written about the effects of reminiscence and all have pointed out how a noticeable array of positive side-effects are fanning out from the procedure, side-effects which in the opinion of Humanitas might well be considered primary effects. In this light Kemp researched the possibilities whether reminiscence activities might cause a break-through in the isolation of the elderly, and how it could improve the relationship with personnel. He compared a scenario where people were shown a video of the past, and one where people were made to talk about the past (i.e. even without the help of museum objects – h.b.). It became obvious that people found pleasure in reminiscing, reminiscence giving the conversation a more spontaneous character, and that it could well be a perfect vehicle for the communication between the elderly and others. An increased responsiveness from the elderly could clearly be established, just as the use of multi-sensory stimuli could intensify the experience. Bender, Bauckham and Norris made similar remarks about reminiscence activities not merely generating measurable effects. They mentioned no less than twenty "side-effects" of reminiscence, thus proving its significance. Amongst others, they mentioned the stimulation of spontaneous conversation, the re-acquirement of forgotten skills, a more in-depth diagnostic process,

and an improved understanding of the client by personnel.

Duncan Cameron has already justified the existence of the reminiscence museum from the way the elderly are prone to collect conversation pieces in their own homes, for themselves and for visitors, in an attempt to create their own little reminiscence museums: "Thus, in their rooms, we find extensive collections of memorabilia and souvenirs, photographs and keepsakes; they have structured them in their attempt to maintain belief in a reality they once perceived but which is, in fact, long passed. It becomes clear, then, that the collection as a reality model serves the collector first and may aid or deter not only the objective perceptions of the collector but also the perceptions of the visitor."

Likewise, the paradigm shift in the reminiscence museum from seeing the client as a subject of care and "expertology", to approaching the client as a worth-while human being with a life-story and communicational skills, dialogues and stories, is perfectly in keeping with the humanistic endeavour to reclaim the existential world from the systematic world through cultural reproduction, social integration and socialization. And the reminiscence museum is the perfect instrument to achieve this. Openness, receptivity and sensitivity are the catch-words here. Especially in the reminiscence museum there is empathy for the diversity of people and their vulnerabilities. The transitory nature of objects and old rituals, by rights, tend to emphasize the vulnerability of life. Habermas' plea for communication between people, groups and the care organization to take place in a power-free ambiance has literally taken shape in the reminiscence museum. Here, as a counteraction for loneliness, the necessary time will be created: time for attention, time for contact, time for reflection, in combination with accessibility, closeness and a constant renewal in design. This, too, being an aspect of the creative and positive, people-focussed culture within Humanitas, is clearly and implicitly inspired by the core-values of humanism, and a fine example of the workings of the humanistic approach.

Great grandchildren visiting the reminiscence museum in the care centre

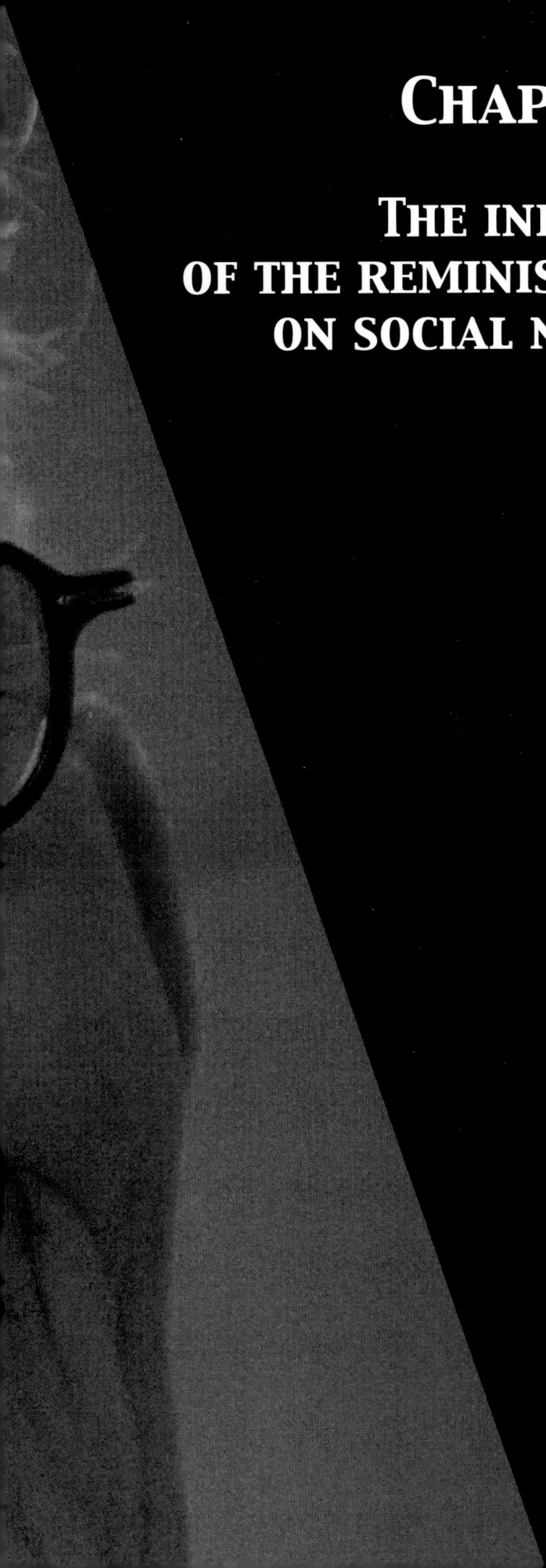

Chapter 4

The influence of the reminiscence museum on social networking

Orange-decorated room of the seventies

THE INFLUENCE OF THE REMINISCENCE MUSEUM ON SOCIAL NETWORKING

The museum, as stated before, has a connecting function, bringing various groups together in what might be called caring, warm communities. The Dutch Board of Social Development suggests in her advice , under the heading "Millions of people being lonely together" the extreme importance of realizing community care. This, in fact, does not only involve organizing the care, but organizing the community as well. From the information received from people living outside the care organization it might be concluded that they, any advantages of living independently aside, experience loneliness as one of the major downsides. A reminiscence museum has the advantage of providing people outside, as well as inside the organization, with a new social network. The "International Council of Museums" describes the function of a museum as being a permanent institution servicing the community and her development, accessible to the public, not intent on financial gain, and collects, stores, performs scientific research, and exhibits the material testimonies of man and his surroundings, and supplies information for the purpose of study, education, and pleasure. As stated before, in the case of the reminiscence museum, which might be considered a community museum prototype, the latter – the pleasure – is at the top of the list. Not only the personal pleasure, but in particular the shared pleasure experience. Aside from the material points of contact from the past, the museum provides a connection for the immaterial testimonies from the public as well. The "collecting" and "storing" are clearly not a major issue, but "scientific research" and "purposes for study", however, are available in abundance, directly or indirectly, considering the fact that so little is known of the effects the combination of objects, smells, sounds and pictures might have on the wellbeing of clients, or on the creation of a new social network.

Animal and pets, like museumobjects, are perfect conversation pieces. In the reminiscence museum Bergweg we have a Moroccan shed with a donkey and a goat. This camel, carrying the author's Turkish partner, thought it necessary to lose at least 20 litres of liquid amidst about a thousand party guests. Great hilarity and enough conversation pieces to last for a long time

In any case, the reminiscence museum appears to be a perfect vehicle to supply people inside and outside the care organisation with fresh social contacts. This is important. Loneliness as a consequence of social isolation, in relation to one's perception of the degree of isolation of the people in one's surroundings, is very relevant indeed and hard to overcome. The death of loved ones, broken relationships, life-rhythm restricting physical disabilities, decline of mobility, and as well as alienation with a multi-ethnic society, tend to turn the elderly into a vulnerable group where loneliness is concerned. Next to the extended family approach, combined with the yes-culture, the restaurants, exhibitions, parties and pets, the reminiscence museum is a perfect vehicle to promote the establishment of new senior-citizen groups, and a new social network. When Csíkszentmihály poses that "flow (the 'being active' which brings happiness – h.b.) is generally reported when a person is doing his or her favourite activity", he is referring to gardening, making music, doing sports, or cooking. Csíkszentmihály is, of course, not familiar with the recent Humanitas development of the reminiscence museum, the regular visits of which could even be more beneficial to our elderly clients than the abovementioned activities he mentioned.

It also works for clients with dementia, we are pleased to say. When a demented lady, who really

has lost the faculty of coherence, suddenly sits down on the plush armchair in the living room of the thirties and very clearly announces: "I am home", it not only moves the bystanders and the accompanying carer, but also opens the door for some degree of future activity training with the lady. When another visitor with dementia suddenly discovers the wooden rattle and starts to have a go at it, while her friends join her in a rattle-melody, this might be – for this category – what Csíkszentmihály would consider to be "flow". The incident had such an impact on the lady, she refused to relinquish the rattle. We then lovingly gave it to her as a present, and she returned to her nursing home room a very happy lady.
Professor Ten Bosch, when addressing the quality systems in the care industry, mentions that the clients' major issues are sometimes not addressed, and we heartily agree with him when he states that in his opinion: "quality should always supersedes the mechanisms procedures, regulations, techniques etc. Those operations do not guarantee quality. Quality, as I see it, is what is added to a product by people who use their hearts". The reminiscence museum proves to be a marketplace for a large variety of people, clients, family, personnel and volunteers, who are, as in some kind of communal museum séance, simultaneously emphatic and create a variety of connections. In the first place there is the bonding between the generations within one family. Father, mother, children, grandchildren and sometimes further generations, are offered a tool for bonding and commu-

Use it or lose it: father Becker (photo left) painting his own house at the age of 89, mother Becker inspecting her brandnew car at the age of 91

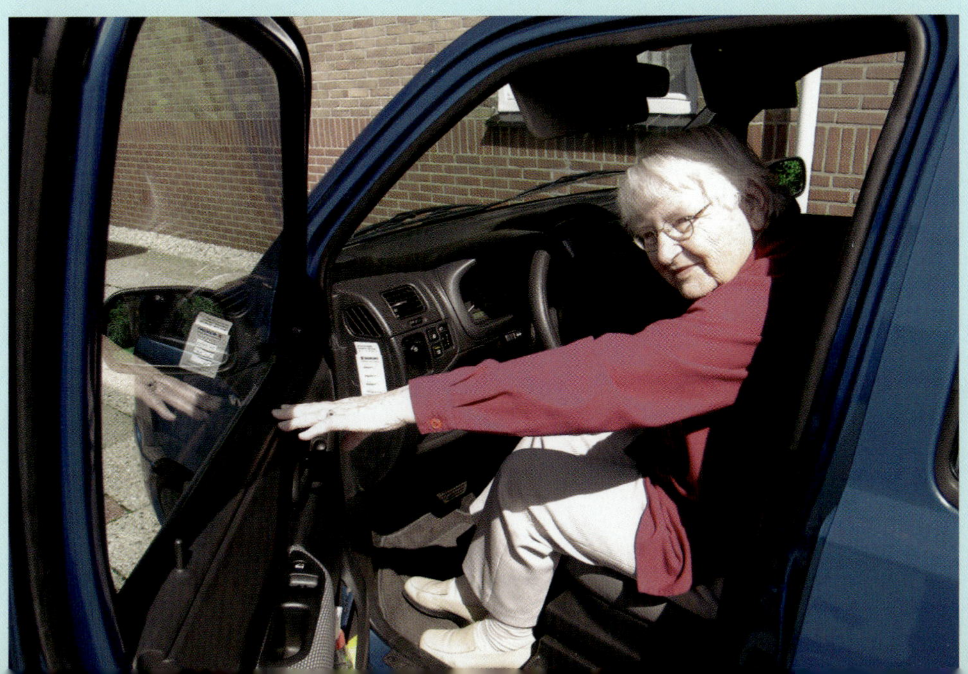

The Rotterdam Town Hall in the middle of a totally destructed Rotterdam centre after the air raid in the second world war.

nication, having a laugh together and have better understanding. When great-grandmother explains to her eldest grandson how she suffered at the dentist, who used a pedal-operated drill (see page 68) in the same way a sewing machine was operated, this creates a bond. The offspring suddenly understand why those old folk can be so miserly at times (caused by for instance the recession, the winter of starvation, and the thrifty reconstruction years). Furthermore, skills and professions from the past and present meet up with each other. Young carpenters are dumbfounded at what the elderly ones managed to accomplish with often very primitive tools. They are also amazed at the ingenuity of the tools of olden days.
Extensive discussions with total strangers often end up by having a cup of coffee together, or even to meet up to visit another museum.
Alma Wittlin rightly states: "Museums are man-made institutions in the service of men; they are not ends in themselves". Strengthening the social network is, therefore, the outcome of a consciously created situation.
As clients of the care institution are engulfed by a stream of visitors from outside because of the reminiscence museum, here again a symbiosis is

The same place 10 years later

born. Visitors from other parts of the town, or neighbouring towns, will find their roots again and while discussing the objects, photographs, films and paintings, will automatically be drawn back to their place of birth, the old school, or their wedding. A painting picturing a destructed Rotterdam during the war, and another one of the same area ten years later, will surely get the stories going. As a matter of fact, the well-known regulations of any museum are opposed to those of the reminiscence museum, in that they stipulate, according to Duncan Cameron: "Don't touch anything, don't get excited, don't take pictures, don't laugh out loud". The ban on touching in our case is turned around into a ban on **not** touching, which explains the choice for the title of this work. Last, but not least, there is the encouragement of the extended family-feeling between clients and personnel. As they get a chance in the museum to get acquainted in another way, rather than the problem-related top-down way which is so common to care institutions, different and more pleasant relationships can evolve. The role of the museum is really the consequence of what Maines formulates as the never-ending daily search of people how to interpret their past. "Symbolic reconstruction of the past involves redefining the meaning of previous events so as to render them meaningful and useful for the present", whereby the museum facilitates the re-interpretation of the past in terms of in-depth intensity and different aspects. If the museum has tools on display to help with the sugar beet harvest, it will remind the one of the Dutch "hunger-winter" when even beetroots were consumed, the other of the painful financial struggle between sugarcane and sugarbeet, and a third will be reminded of the terribly muddy roads during harvest time. The total sum of material and immaterial events is an enhancement of human bonding, self esteem and subsequent human happiness.

"Why are the elderly so thrifty?" Whatever the cause, poverty in general, the crisis, the winter of starvation of the Second World War, of the thrifty post-war reconstruction, a well known and much used item to ensure survival was the household money box. The examples shown are from the thirties and fifties. The latter has the savings-item "vacation" added to it. By that time the Dutch were rich enough to take a real vacation. Both boxes have "coal" prominently displayed

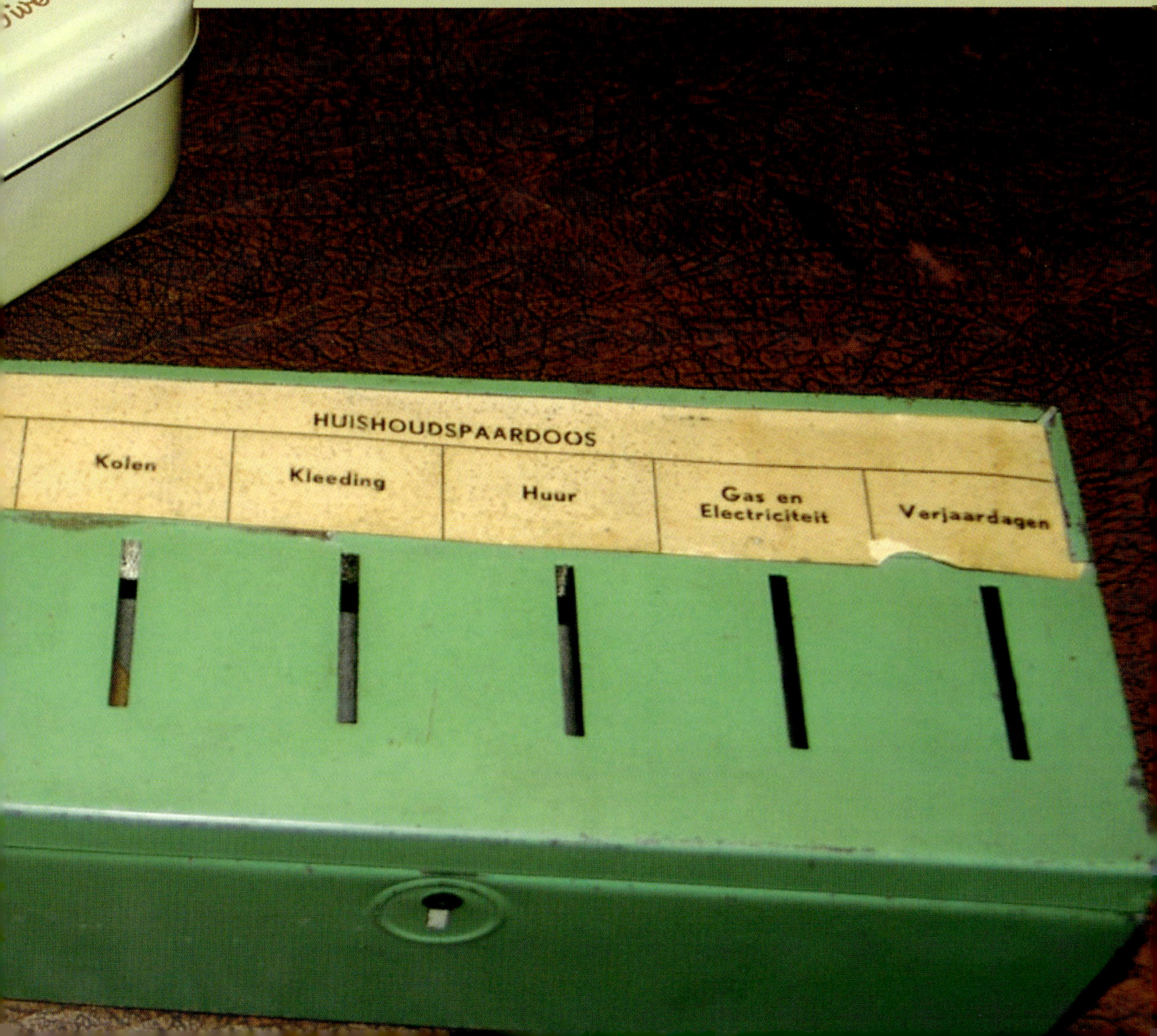

When great grandmother explains to her great grandson about the pain she suffered "at the hands" of the pedal-pushed dentist's drill, it will no doubt give a connection. This dental chair (1930) was donated to Humanitas by a regional community museum

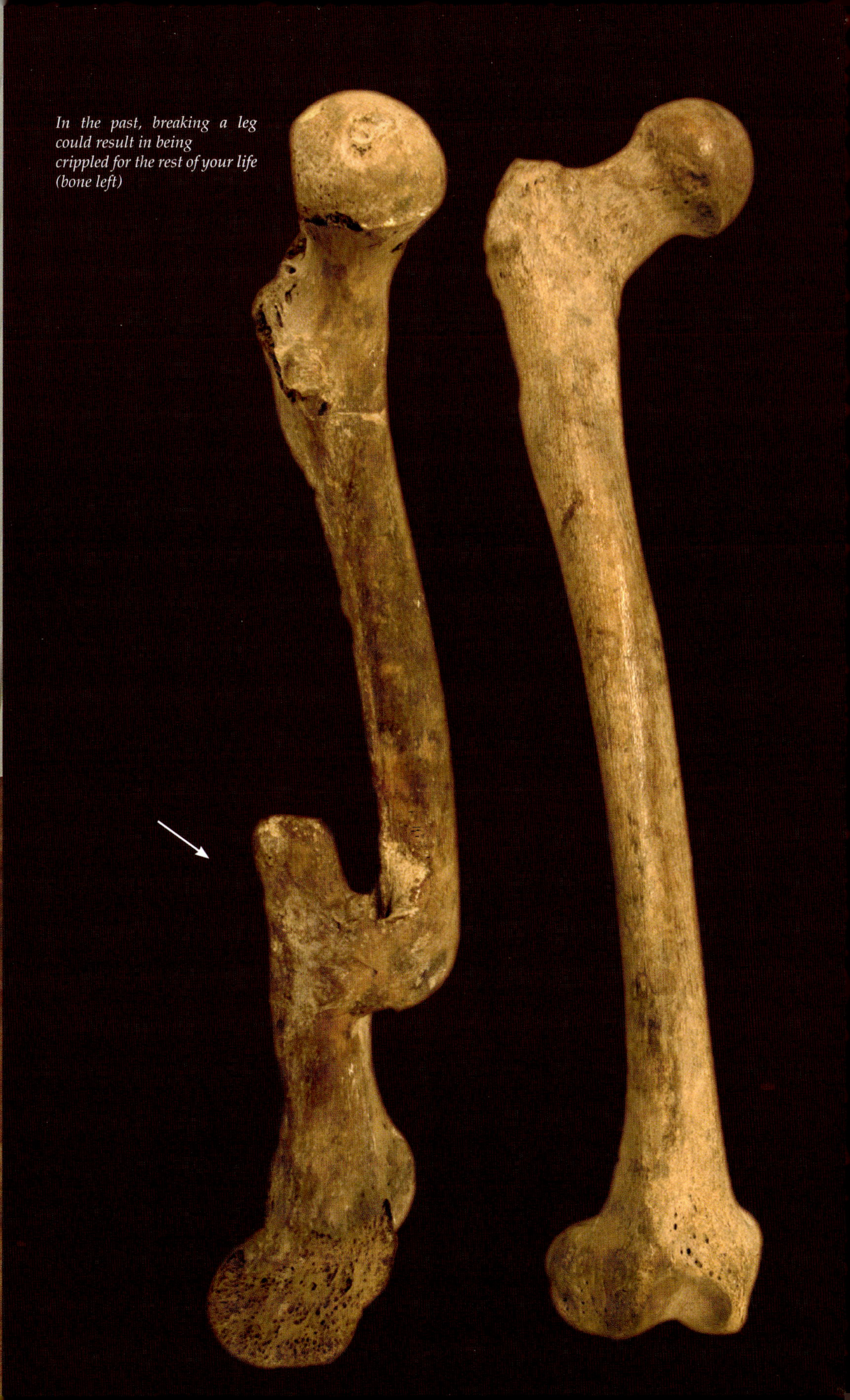

In the past, breaking a leg could result in being crippled for the rest of your life (bone left)

Chapter 5

How to successfully employ volunteer workers in the reminiscence museum

A special element of the reminiscence museum is the dedication of the, mostly elderly, volunteer workers. The museum offers an array of volunteer tasks: security-attendants, guards, museum attendants, purchasers, restorers, cleaners, documentation researchers, funding experts, pr-speci-

Museum volunteer workers are mainly recruited from the category of "the silent generation" , born between 1930 – 1945. Having spent their youths during war time, but mainly formed by the post-war reconstruction, they may be characterized as hard workers who feared grandeur. Here we see the museum-volunteer force of Humanitas-Akropolis in Rotterdam

alist, etc., many tasks of which are naturally blended together.
There are a number of aspects to consider when using these dedicated volunteer workers: the impact it has on the visitors, on the volunteer workers themselves, on the economical revenue, the impact on the growth of the collection and the attention it requires for the right training and attitude of the volunteer workers. The publication "Ageing, or Ageing with a Silver Lining" already mentions that senior citizens themselves feel they are able to make a valuable contribution, having so much expertise and experience available. The volunteer workers at the reminiscence museum are clearly living proof of this. These volunteers are mainly recruited from

the group, referred to by sociologist Becker "the silent generation" (born between 1930 and 1945), and characterized as: childhood during the war, but especially identified as the generation of the post-war reconstruction years - hard workers and fearful of grandeur. They have great affinity with the group of reminiscence visitors, in a social-cultural context. They have their life experiences and – literally – the images of an era, in common.

An important point is that the volunteer attendants, often donating objects themselves, cleaning them and putting them on display, are not intent on financial gain. They have become specialists by all the stories of the public and by their own experiential expertise, acting more as an audience and story-reciprocating guide, rather than as attendants. They are clearly working for their own personal happiness and pleasure. According to Joris van Pruyenbroeck, the elaborating audience – meaning inter-active listeners facilitating reminiscence – will enable the reminiscing speaker to elaborate on a memory. They affirm the memory and elaborate on certain details, by posing relevant questions. Thus - acting as a worthy citizen - being an attendant will create human happiness for the volun-

No shouting into the client's ear from behind the wheelchair, but positioning yourself in front of the client is the right way for a volunteer attendant to make contact with the client via the object

The guided tours for elderly with dementia require special skills from the attendant, such as sensitivity to, and empathy for the (former) lifestyle of the visitor

teer workers themselves. In the meantime, this human happiness is being passed on to the visitors. It is obviously important to visitors to have their questions answered and the visit will enhance in intensity and human warmth. Less obvious, but maybe even more important – and so unlike regular museums – is the fact that by listening and asking open questions, clients may be activated to reminisce and recount their memories. The volunteer workers must, therefore, receive training to listen attentively and ask open questions. Should this not be effective, it will do no harm if the attendants tell a story themselves. Certainly with large groups this might entice people to come forward with stories of their own.

For a volunteer worker, acting as attendant in a reminiscence museum could be the answer to a life of monotony and boredom. There is always something new to talk about, if only because the collection is continually replenished, and by the diversity of the visiting public with their own amazing stories and remarks. Besides, the work also includes doing small repair work, polishing and cleaning the objects, which might result in a very pleasant group effort.

Ekodur
Ekodur

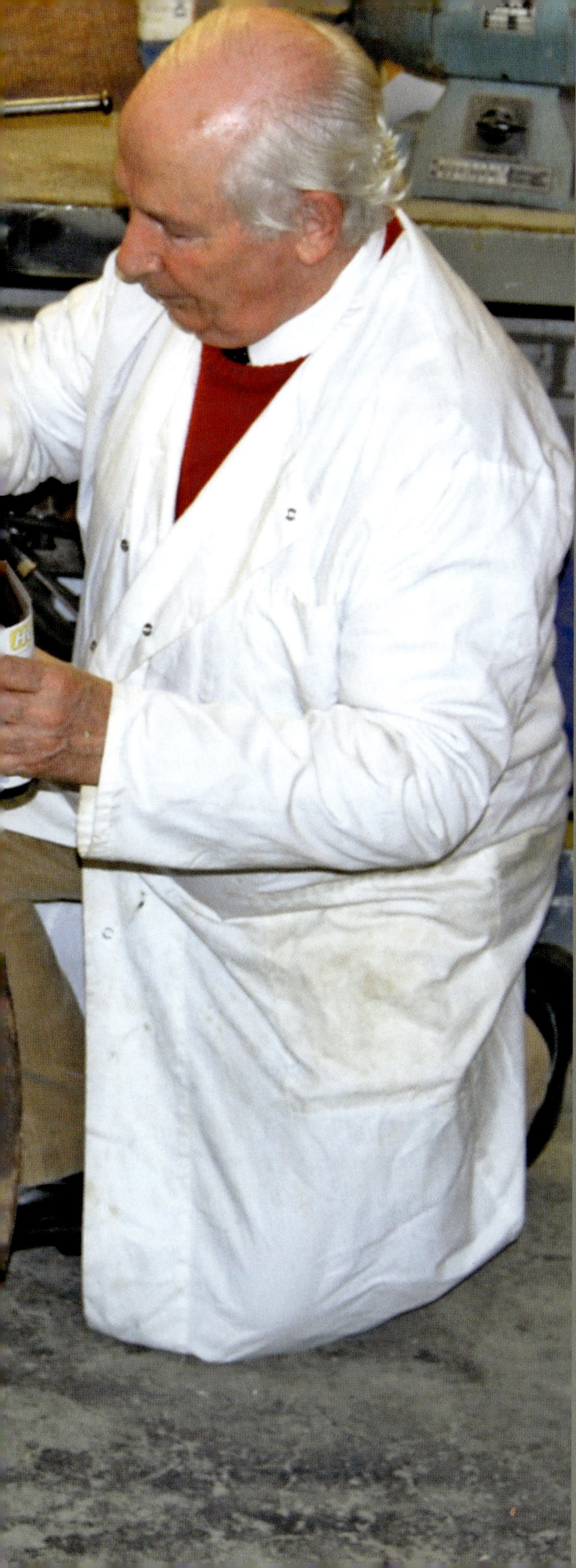

The volunteer workers themselves have a magnet-function for the donation of new objects for the collection. This takes place by "word-of-mouth" advertising in their own small circle , but also by enquiring "in a roundabout way" whether visitors have any worthwhile objects lying around to donate to the museum. Maybe small objects, like savings-stamps, or -coupons from bygone days (the Dutch were known for their thrifty saving mania), and which are highly appreciated by the museum public: "Oh, I used to save those too!".

The use of dedicated volunteer workers also results, after the initial expenditure for lay-out and equipment, in an extremely low-cost running of the museum. Labour, always the major part of the expenditures in the elderly care, will now be as good as covered.
Taking dementia clients on a guided tour requires a number of special skills from the volunteer attendant. To some extent these skills can be mastered, but for the rest

Museum restorers should not try to restore items "as new"; the wear and tear of time should still be visible they are due to character. The core values are patience and the sensitivity to be imaginative about the (former) lifestyle of the visitor. Imagining what would interest and attract each visitor individually, including dementia clients. For example, they might be materials, and flat-irons, when the visitor used to be an ironing maid. Feeling the materials and the starched collars and handling the iron would then become very important. Evoking a reaction through sounds, like the sound of the electric sewing machine, or the songs from that era, will have a similar result. Merely setting up a signpost in the middle of a lawn saying "bus-stop", or a randomly placed telephone booth, thinking this might be fun for the demented is, in my opinion, nonsensical. Objects and sounds should be the real thing and be displayed, in an inter-active way, as an entire package.

The handi(wo)men and restorers should be aware not to try and fix the objects to "look as new". The touch of time should be still recognizable in a reminiscence museum. Run-down and worn-out objects will in fact conjure up the most memories by way of their wear, the trouble and strife of the past they stand for.

And so the knife cuts both ways. On the one hand, the on average more than twenty volunteer workers a reminiscence museum has on staff have created for themselves an extensive social network, which constantly renews itself and guarantees long-lasting happiness. On the other hand, the volunteer workers will enhance emotions and evoke new (reminiscence) emotions. It cannot be emphasized enough how invigorating the role of volunteer workers can be. Their presence and willingness to engage in conversation with visitors are indispensable components for

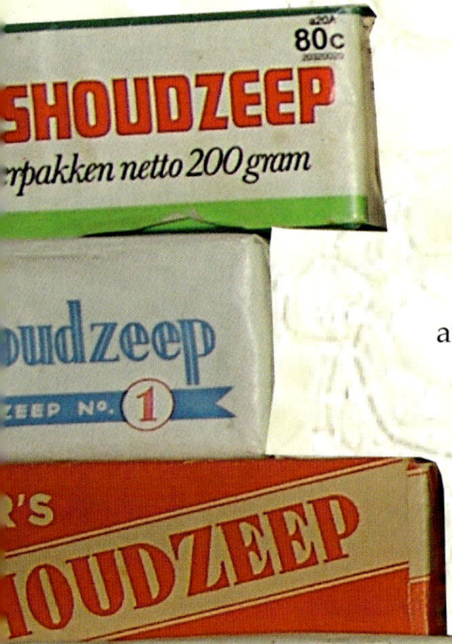

Roodzegel
een super kwaliteit
HUISHOUDZEEP
HEMA
3 stukken
375 gram
huishoud
SUNLIGHT
SAVON
Castella
HOUDZEEP
No 1
DE BESTE EN GOEDKOOPSTE HUIS
ZUINIG IN GEBRU
CONDOR
ZEEP
GLORI
klokzeep
huishoudzeep / nettogewicht 200 gram bij het verpakken
STOOMZEEPFABRIEK
Het Klaverblad N.V.
SUNLIGHT
ZEEP
ECHTE
ZUIVERE ZEEP
HET BESTE VOOR
ALLES WAT SCHOON MOET
SHOUD
No 1
Goedgekeurd door de
Nederlandse Vereniging
van Huisvrouwen.
HEMA
zeep
SEIFE
SUNLIGHT ZEEP

the success of the reminiscence museum. Fact is also, that the volunteer workers and visitors are often from the same generation, which facilitates a ready and easy contact.

One could categorize museum volunteer workers in what I have called in my Volunteer Worker Index (see annexe) "social network / pastime seekers", whereby the pastime-volunteer who is merely trying to spend his time in a useful and pleasant way, is in the majority. There are, of course, other categories, like the loneliness-volunteer. The clock restorer might be called a "use it or lose it"-volunteer, the curator an idealist-volunteer, and the handyman a volunteer who likes to learn a new trade. But whatever backgrounds and agendas the volunteer workers might have, they are enjoying this pleasant and very inspiring work as a team, meanwhile providing so much human happiness to the vulnerable elderly in the last phase of their lives.

Chapter 6

Acquisition of objects, smells, audio and video material

ACQUISITION OF OBJECTS, SMELLS, AUDIO AND VIDEO MATERIAL

The most important sources for acquiring reminiscence objects, aside from findings in dustbins, junk shops, second-life shops, and antique markets, are the gift donations. This kind of acquisition has the advantage of giving us some information about their background. "Mum's old wedding shoes" imply that the exact age of the shoes is known, as well as the social background of their owner. When the donators visit the museum at a later stage, they may even supply us with additional information. This exchange of information is fun for themselves, good for the museum, as well as for the attending audience. On occasion, superfluous objects are donated to us by other museums, like the dentist's chair on page 68 Exchanging objects, once there is enough stock available, might be another possibility. For this reason Humanitas delivered a container of objects to Dutch Care Ltd in Australia.

Before the large stream of gifts and donations will begin to flow naturally, a basic collection needs to be on display, which, in itself, will have a magnet function. The objects already on display clearly influence the willingness to donate. Seeing is donating, you might say. People tend to come up with all sorts of ideas to add to the collection. A care organization with the inclination to set up a reminiscence museum should, therefore, start collecting objects to form a primary collection. When those basic objects are not available in-house, one needs to purchase them. At markets, in antiquity and antique shops, at fairs and jumble sales, second-life shops, auctions, etc. There is also the possibility to search for missing items on-line (e-bay for instance). And a pot of glue from the fifties will then be found in no time. Having connections with junk shops and second-life shops is very important as the items are not only reasonably priced, but the shop assistants – volunteer workers themselves - are often very interested to help. They will co-operate and plan ahead,

Enamelled bill boards to enrich the objects on display will cause emotions to soar

...lum's " lovingly and frequently cobbled old wedding shoes, donated by the 86-year old owner, means that the ... and social background of these shoes can be established

keeping goods from being sold to others, and hanging on to un-sellable items, such as old garments or darned socks, which are so precious to the museum, and to save them for the museum instead.

Objects, such as old shoes, and toys, which have been repaired and restored over and over again, are of much more interest to the museum, than the same objects which for some reason have been kept in pristine condition. More often than not, the dedicated team of purchasing-volunteers of the reminiscence museum will do the rounds on the second hand-life shops themselves, thus playing a very different role from the volunteer attendants. Of course there are many more ways to acquire objects for the museum, such as free advertising on the notice boards at supermarkets, on the local and in-house television circuits or in personnel bulletins, local and regional papers, and even putting up posters inside the museum, all excellent means for promotion. Organizing a photo-quiz in the regional paper of rare, or unusual objects from the past: “Remember this one?” (with a Humanitas dinner voucher award for the winner), will do great to promote the museum to a wider public. It is invariably interesting to observe the reactions it invokes, and how it will trigger people to come up with ideas to add to the collection. Donations such as the inheritance of the complete household inventory of someone’s hundred year old aunt,

A pot of paste-glue from the sixties, including paste brushes, can still be procured on e-Bay with little effort

Second-life shops, once befriended, tend not to throw away un-sellable items such as darned socks, but instead save them for the museum. Here a pair of socks, with several darning eggs

who never threw away anything. Granddad 's old moped, complete with instructions, as good as new, and kept by the family for over thirty years out of respect, as well as great grandfather's long-johns which somehow never found their way to the dustbin, they all find their way to the museum. But there is more. One needs more than the mere display of objects to make it work. A 1920 bicycle with wooden wheel-frames on display, accompanied by an old photograph of that very bicycle amidst twenty others on a ferry into town, adds in emotional value. Add to this the smell of the rubber solution to repair the tires with, the sound of the bicycle bell, and the music from an old cycling inspired evergreen, and it will put the whole scene into context. Putting the objects on display into context is so very important. For instance with visual aids: photographs, posters, old movies need to be found to accompany the objects, to make memories even more vivid. To that end the Humanitas reminiscence museum in Rotterdam has come to an excellent understanding with the city's Historical Museum, as well as its War Memorial Museum, the City Archives, and various regional museums. Accompanying sounds are easy to reproduce, or may be extracted from, for instance, old radio broadcasts. The bombardment of Rotterdam, displayed with photographs and objects, will clearly be more frightening and, therefore, more memory-inducing, when accompanied by the sound of the drone of over-flying aeroplanes, and the chilling sound of airraid alarm in 1940. The painting of the devastation of a bombarded Rotterdam, and another picturing the reconstruction (the Lijnbaan) as shown on page 65 will give the scene an extra dimension, and cause the visitors to reflect in nostalgia. After which some kind of eruption of anecdotes and war recollections is bound to follow. Scents and smells are usually best recreated by using the original scent evoking objects again: For instance the fragrances of old perfumes, the unmistakable smells of solution, moth balls, bee wax, cod liver oil, carbide, real soap suds, aniseed, chicory, and real onions, etc. It is a question of trial and error, and some effort on the part of the volunteer workers, before getting it right.

One last addition to the spectre of objects, visual aids, sounds and smells, are the accompanying tastes. Aniseed sweets, home made fudge, liquorice, sour balls and maybe home-made crumpets, but also marmite, golden syrup, etc. Dishes from the kitchen of old can be reproduced too. It goes without saying that here one needs the help of volunteer-chefs who, by using recipes from old cookery books and with the advice from elderly customers, can bring those old-fashioned dishes back to life. It is quite interesting to observe how a menu from bygone days will create an unforgettable atmosphere at a ninetieth, or hundredth birthday party, and intensify the memories of the occasion.

Scents and smells are usually best recreated by using the original scent evoking objects again: For instance the scents of old perfumes, the unmistakable smells of solution, moth balls, bee wax, cod liver oil, carbide, real soap suds, aniseed, chicory, and real onions, etc

A typically Dutch "Solex" moped from grandfather's time, including the user's manual, found its way to the reminiscence museum

A purchased leaded glass picture pane now adorns the atrium of the Humanitas-Akropolis building and adds grandeur to the hall

Acquisition of atmosphere defining and informative leaded glass picture panes (these items are rarely donated) can be very important. As gifts they would be highly appreciated. The ones shown here were a gift from a grateful family

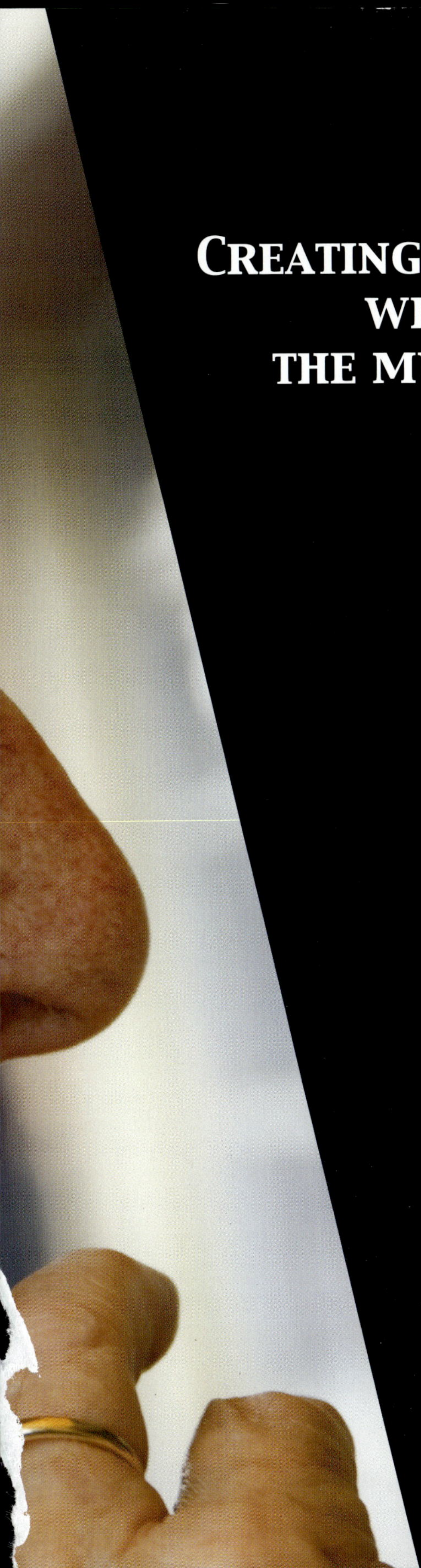

Chapter 7

Creating the necessary space: where to situate the museum collection?

The author and mrs. Ros looking over their first "catch" of reminiscence items. Storage space, to a museum, is as important as the space to exhibit

CREATING THE NECESSARY SPACE: WHERE TO SITUATE THE MUSEUM COLLECTION?

Like most other museums, a reminiscence museum uses up a large number of square metres. Not only to accommodate the display of the objects, but also for extra room to move around in a wheelchair, and to store the donated objects. Moreover, library space needs to be provided for to accommodate the many books which will undoubtedly become part of the collection. In the case of contemporary buildings, their space so carefully calculated, this may prove to be quite a challenge.

Older buildings, despite all the usual disadvantages, have space as a clear advantage. Vast spaces in the basement, formerly used for transport and storage but on account of modern logistics left empty, or stocked with superfluous rubbish, are perfect for the purpose. Large hallways and wide corridors, often not found in modern buildings, are also perfectly usable.

In the case of modern buildings, using part of the parking garage to house the museum might be an option, or maybe parts of the communal areas inside, where the lack of daylight will exclude a large number of other activities anyway. The lack of daylight can sometimes be an advantage for a reminiscence museum, as lighting may then be adjusted according to need.

Actually, a reminiscence museum does not always need to be set up in a separate area. Displays in the lobby, the hallways and corridors, the boardrooms and visitor areas will do perfectly. The in-house supermarket will be fine to display a collection of tins, jars and bottles, scales, milk cans, household soaps etc., without the loss of valuable space, or money. Thus, the created atmosphere of a rustic village shop will add to the pleasure of the elderly shopper. Boardrooms, provided they allow enough room to place objects, cupboards, or cabinets alongside the walls, are perfectly suitable. A collection will also add to the ambiance of the room. In this way, a multi-functional board room proves to be a useful asset during the times in between meetings. The same goes for restaurants. A good restaurant needs a theme. It is not just about the choice of dishes on the menu and the service provided, but there should be ambiance, too. Like the Humanitas restaurant "The Elated Elephant", where elephants in all shapes

Even a contemporary supermarket could put tins, jugs, scales and bottles from the past on display, and it would not use up much space or money, but would do much to improve the ambiance

Old pharmacy with a volunteer-attendant reminiscence museum Humanitas-Bergweg

HACKS
HACKS
HACKS

Older buildings, despite their obvious disadvantages, clearly have space as an advantage. Vast basement areas, formerly used for storage and transport are nowadays, on account of improved logistics, either partly or completely empty, or stocked with superfluous rubbish. They would be perfect for creating a reminiscence museum

and sizes, and made from all kinds of materials are part of the decorations, or another restaurant where a theme of butterflies accentuate its name, in the same way a museum restaurant, decorated with objects from the museum, will enhance the ambiance. A visit to the museum could even be combined with a matching restaurant menu of old-fashioned dishes to accentuate the theme even more.

Old leaded glass windows, so typical for the era, with their warm colours and often fetching images will generally be excellent to conjure up the atmosphere and ambiance inside the museum itself. And ambiance is a prerequisite in a reminiscence museum, if the appearance of a junk-shop is to be avoided. The ice-floe shaped pieces of "antique" glass, discolouring the daylight to a typical and rather murky hue, are therefore excellent to be used as prefix windows to break the harshness of the cold and pure light of our contemporary windows. An interesting feature when using glass show cases throughout the museum is that the objects on display, when placed in front of a glazed outside wall, seem to connect the inside with the outside world. By looking at the objects from the inside, one automatically looks at the outside world, and vice versa. When the care

Separate rooms are not always necessary. Museum objects may also be displayed along those typically spacious institution's corridors, as seen here in one of our Humanitas buildings, with interaction with the outside

Although the collection does not have many items of value, nowadays it makes sense to install security cameras inside exhibition areas, linked to the reception desk. Once the objects are in your possession, it is only sensible to hold on to them and thiefs cause much damage

centre is regarded as some kind of sheltered village square within the neighbourhood, it could be advantageous to use this feature to invoke the interest, and entice the outside public to enter. Museum objects tend to invoke curiosity, and lower the threshold-feeling.

Although the objects in a collection are usually not very valuable, it would be sensible in this day and age to make adequate provisions to keep the spaces locked and install CCTV, linked to the reception desk. The financial damage to doors and show cases is often more extensive than the damage incurred by the stolen goods, and the disruption caused by a burglary, and the subsequent feeling of insecurity for the volunteer workers and visitors – not to mention the effect it will have on the inhabitants with all the fuss and commotion – is substantial. When something does happen, it is advisable to play it down and avoid any publicity. Generally speaking, insuring the collection is not an option, in view of the high premium payments, the low costs of acquisition and easy replacement of the museum objects.

Museum restaurant

'Sweet Memories'

Starters

Beetroot soup
Sauerkraut soup with smoked sausage

Main courses

Mashed apple and potato pie
baked cow's udder
Fried pig's ears
Braised beef, Brussels sprouts and boiled potatoes
Fried slices of black pudding
braised herring with salad

Desserts

Semolina porridge with bilberry sauce
sweetened buttermilk pudding
Pudding with treacle

A "Sweet memories" menu with typical Dutch dishes from days gone by

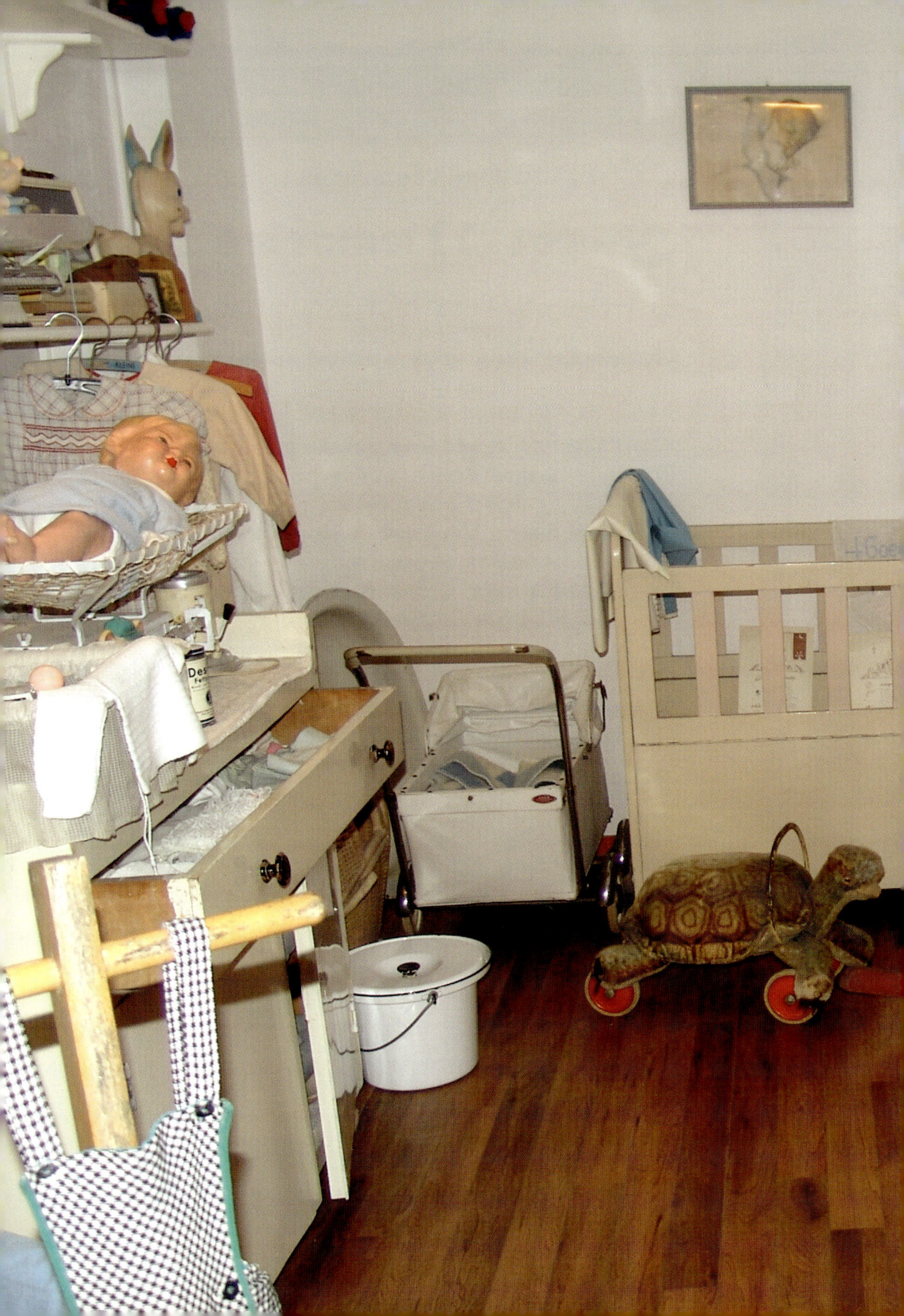

Children's room including (dr. Spocks' childraising manual)

Chapter 8

How to design a display of objects

HOW TO DESIGN A DISPLAY OF OBJECTS

However attractive it may be for the atmosphere and ambiance to have a few really fine items in the collection, such as a large, century-old oak table in the lobby, a splendid cabinet, or a few exquisite paintings – after all, every household was bound to have one or more valuable items in its possession – expensive items are not usually what matters to the reminiscence museum. Rare objects of value, from the point of view of reminiscence, are often of less importance than more ordinary, everyday household objects, such as a well worn old leather jacket. These are usually donated to the museum in large quantities. The bulk of donations received by Humanitas on a monthly basis, is generally about half a cubic metre. So when something breaks, or is lost, it is not the end of the world. The element of conservation, so eminent in most museums, is not a major feature in a reminiscence museum. Also the fact that the educational aspect is, obviously, of less importance, has its consequences. For instance, information signposts should be kept to a minimum. With the exception maybe of a slogan we once encountered at the NEMO Science Centre in Amsterdam, and which we have declared applicable for the reminiscence museum: "Hands off not an option!". One of the few signs allowed to be shown, as far as we are concerned. Visitors are best left to figure things out for themselves, or put their questions to fellow visitors, thereby engaging in interaction. A attitude completely opposed to the regular museums, where touching is strictly forbidden (as one Dutch Folk singer from the sixties, singing about dating put it: "You may just look, but never touch"), and where information is often supplied in a rather intrusive way. After all, the aim of the reminiscence museum is to have fun - fun in reminiscence, fun in the search for history and background, fun in sharing these memories with others, fun in re-acquainting oneself with the objects and thereby reliving the memory, fun in creating a family feeling on account of a commonly shared history. The wedding photos, wooden ice-skates, and formal attire of the past will baffle the younger generation and create a pleasant and interested atmosphere.

The objects should in any case be placed in such a way as to allow wheelchair owners access. They need to be able to see, touch and handle the objects as well. The tray for potato peelings, and the pail, should be within reach. The chord-bell ought to be on wheelchair level and, likewise, the scoop to ladle out beans from the container. It is also fun for the (great)

However attractive it might be to have some really fine antiques on display, such as a large hundred-year old oak table in the lobby, or an old masterpiece, like the "Man peeling potatoes " shown here, expensive items are not really of importance to the reminiscence museum

grandchildren to have the wooden cart, the scooter with the funny pot-helmet, the moped, the stilts and rocking horse displayed in such a way that they are easy to climb on and play with. The enjoyment will be as real as fifty years ago. And please do not forget to hand out some butterscotch and fudge to the youngest generation.
A special aspect which might sometimes be tricky, is the wish of some visitors to retrieve the items donated by them. "Where is our cookery book? Where did you put our Singer sewing machine?" But what if there are already fifty donated sewing machines, and dozens of cookery books? So, on the one hand a uniformity of the simple, everyday household goods is an advantage. The objects are so similar, one hardly notices the difference. On the other, Humanitas is in the process of setting up at least five more reminiscence museums, which require many identical objects and people may have to be referred to these sister-museums.
Another aspect which requires attention is the lighting. Elderly visitors need much light to see properly. Turning the museum into a show case with bright fluorescent lighting where people do not feel comfortable, however, should be avoided. A shed, after all, should retain some of its darkness and mystery. A living room from the thirties had a tendency to look a little bleak and gloomy, if only because society was poor, and energy was expensive. A combination of theme-corners with matching lighting, divided by the well-lit show cases, where hundreds of objects of similar kind are displayed very clearly, is guaranteed to be successful. The volunteer attendants may well use old-fashioned lanterns and dymo torches to light up details in a theme corner, which will add some sense of adventure to the experience.

Great aunt Anna, photographed by the author's father some seventy years ago. Such a picture on the wall of the exhibition area will certainly enhance the atmosphere

Lighting plays a very important part in a display. A shed, by rights, should retain some of its darkness and mystery

Window panes allowing direct daylight are not always an advantage. Often the light is too bright to create a rustic atmosphere. In the old days window panes were relatively expensive, and people were poor, which is why they had small windows. Contemporary large window panes could therefore be boarded off completely, or partially, to make them smaller, or have the light tempered by a prefix window made from (uni- or multi-coloured) leaded glass. Wooden panelling could also be an option, (be it that it should barely be noticeable). Please note that, as with hairdresser's salons, bars and supermarkets, the lighting in the theme-corners and show cases should not be extinguished at the end of the day for economic reasons. It will create a black hole, and rather spoils the atmosphere for the rest of the area. A better option is to use the more expensive LED-lighting, which will earn their keep in no time by saving you money in wages when regular bulbs need replacement. Another important aspect are the walls. As old-fashioned wallpaper is hard to come by, the alternative is to give the walls as little accent as possible. Simple plastering, with a smudge of grey here and there, will act as a perfect background for the objects.

If the objects are being displayed in a chronological timeline, with possible interruptions by former innovations, we recommend you show the timeline in your display. The old shaving knife with blade and sharpening leather could be followed by the first Gillette razor blades (in old times accompanied by a blade-sharpener), in turn to be followed by the first original Philips electric razor (with tall handle, and an old Remington). Which, in turn, started off a subsequent series of more ergonomically shaped models. The first one had just one shaving head, then there was

The author's foster son Mohammed has found some real treasures among the dustbins. We see him here with a genuine "Nordmende Mambino" wireless from the fifties, a needlepoint tapestry featuring children's sing-along songs

the dual shaving head model, after which the three headed model came out. Eventually there was the lady-shave. This visualization of a "creative destruction" series (Schumpeter, economist (1883-1950) already pointed out that innovation is created by the continual process of des-troying old ways of production) will evoke much commentary and nostalgic sighs about the good old days. With the question "which was the first electric razor you used", the volunteer attendant will surely get any man talking. In the same way women react when asked which cookie jar they had in their possession (a cookie jar which was closed demonstratively the moment everyone had had one cookie).
A well designed collection display will give an interesting picture of the development of household objects. If one item in a series of authentic objects can no longer be obtained, there is the possibility to use a replica. But replicas do not really belong in a museum. Especially when we are talking about everyday household objects, the wear and tear are part of the

Antique dolls when touched and handled will be prone to damage. So: keep the real antiques locked in a showcase, and leave the replica dolls, dressed in worn clothes, out to be touched and handled

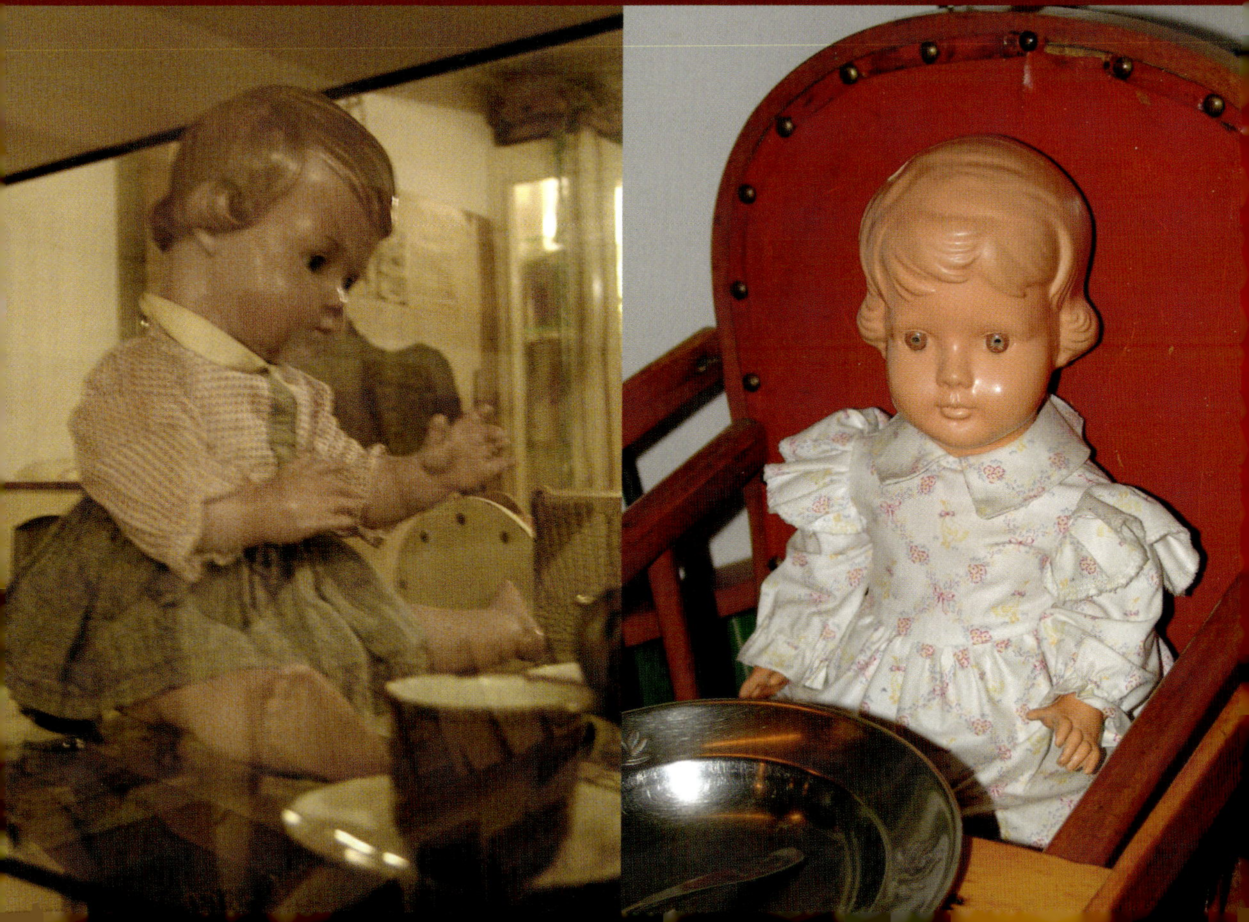

charm. A brand new shaving blade, however well replicated, will always be second to a knife which has its blade worn off to a third of the size from years of wear on the grinding stone. When installing equipment and decorations this ought to be a point of attention as well. A partition made of wooden boards should be constructed from real old planks and when the partition is left unpainted, use old rusty nails (leave the iron nails in water for a few days, by no means use aluminium screws, and if you do, hide them with filler). When repainting a wall, do not go overboard with filler, it should not look brand-new and beautiful, but give an impression of wear and nostalgia. Therefore, the paint is best used with slightly too much thinner, which will give a used and patchy result. There is no need to level and plummet the wall into perfection, people in the old days were known for their botch-jobs!

The attendant's question "Which was the first electric shaver you used?" will get any man talking. A similar effect is seen when women are asked which cookie jar they remember. Such objects should, therefore, be placed together

An exception to the rule of authenticity might be taken in the case of (porcelain) dolls. Displaying antique porcelain dolls to be touched and handled by the public, will increase the risk of breakage. A more doll-friendly construction is to keep the real antique dolls locked in a show case, or cabinet and keep replica dolls, properly smudged and with worn clothes, displayed to be touched and handled.
A special feature to consider are the floor- and wall coverings. A room from the thirties should not be carpeted with material from the sixties. A 1940 toilet ought to have lino on the floor. The shed should have a rough, and worn-out concrete floor, already existing in many basement areas. And the white wall tiles from the sixties in the Humanitas mortuary

were excellent for use in the kitchen theme-room from that era. Kitchens from earlier years needed to be furnished with antique tiles which we purchased. Simple white and black square tiles will suffice nicely for the flooring, and although they may be new, they are hardly distinguishable from the original ones. Incidentally one can come across some old wallpaper, but it is better to work with a smudged and worn-out plastered wall than use something completely at odds with the time.

Ceilings are a problem because it is often too expensive to have original plastered ceilings installed. Fortunately people tend to look down, rather than up, so one can do with a simple prefab ceiling which is also handy when the existing water pipes and wire-circuits above the ceiling of the basement need to be reached. For the shed and laundry room a simple detachable ceiling from wooden boards could be constructed. Fix the beams and slide the boards over them loosely.

Show cases are an integral, but rather expensive part of the museum. So-

The wall tiles from the fifties, used in the former Humanitas mortuary, were excellent for use in the theme kitchen display from the same era

The shed and laundry room are provided with detachable ceilings (simple beams with wooden boards) creating the right "used" impression, but enabling access to the technical installations above

metimes it is possible to convert an old linen cupboard into a show cabinet by removing the doors and replacing them with a glass front. Second hand show cases may also be found in junk shops, or at a jumble sale. But this usually generates one single show case, so constructing a dividing partition made of similar show cases is not possible.

Another fact to take into account: where to initially store all those donated items? They might mean well, but when people arrive with an old Volkswagen van, loaded to the brim with used items, one cannot just leave them in the lobby. Nor can one send the people away. When, as was the case with Humanitas, one has two days to empty the contents of a three story house, where nothing has been changed or altered in over fifty years, one needs to store all the items speedily. So, it is important to create ample storage room, and organize it as efficiently as possible.

Racks against the walls to ceiling height, deep enough to accommodate uniform carton boxes, will ensure that many cubic metres of items can be stored economically. Those very hefty supermarket orange-boxes with grips, are uniform and stackable, and will hold your objects as adequately as the oranges they once held. A customer-friendly supermarket in your neighbourhood will surely lay aside empty boxes for the reminiscence museum. A very important consideration is: who is responsible for the display of the collection? Humanitas learned from practice that their very well-meaning volunteer workers, or others, feel an inclination to add objects, or randomly move objects about, as they see fit. And suddenly an electric fire from the sixties will find its way to the living room of the thirties. In other words: take care the collection does not turn into a jumble sale. Clear and firm arrangements need to be made as to which person will have the overall responsibility to put what where. He, or she, must have some feeling for this. It goes without saying that any contributing ideas are most welcome, but the simple fact is, that being a volunteer worker in a museum does not guarantee you a sense for design, or the ability to organize. Which require different qualifications.

Chapter 9

The pros and cons of sizable and modest facilities

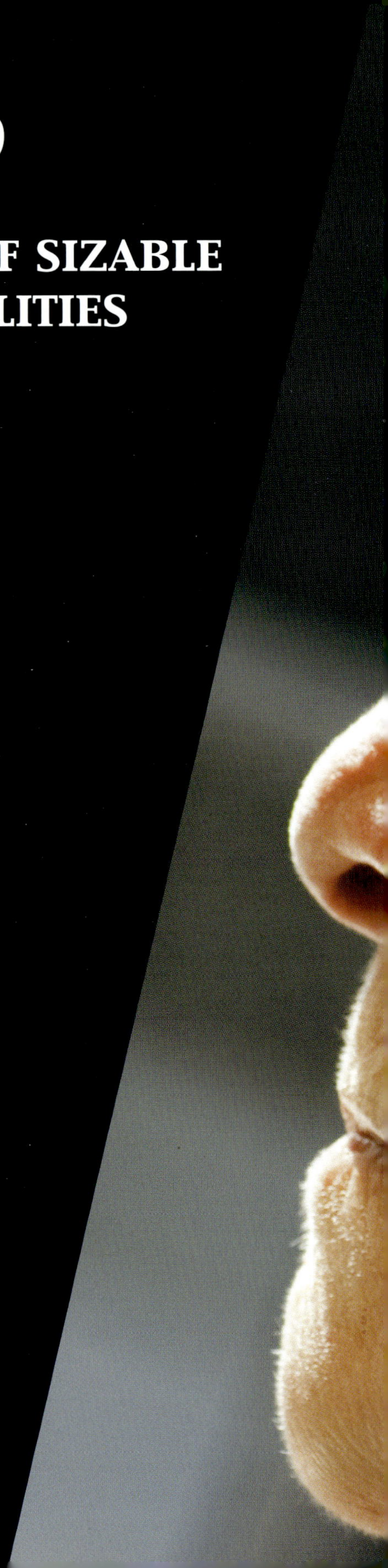

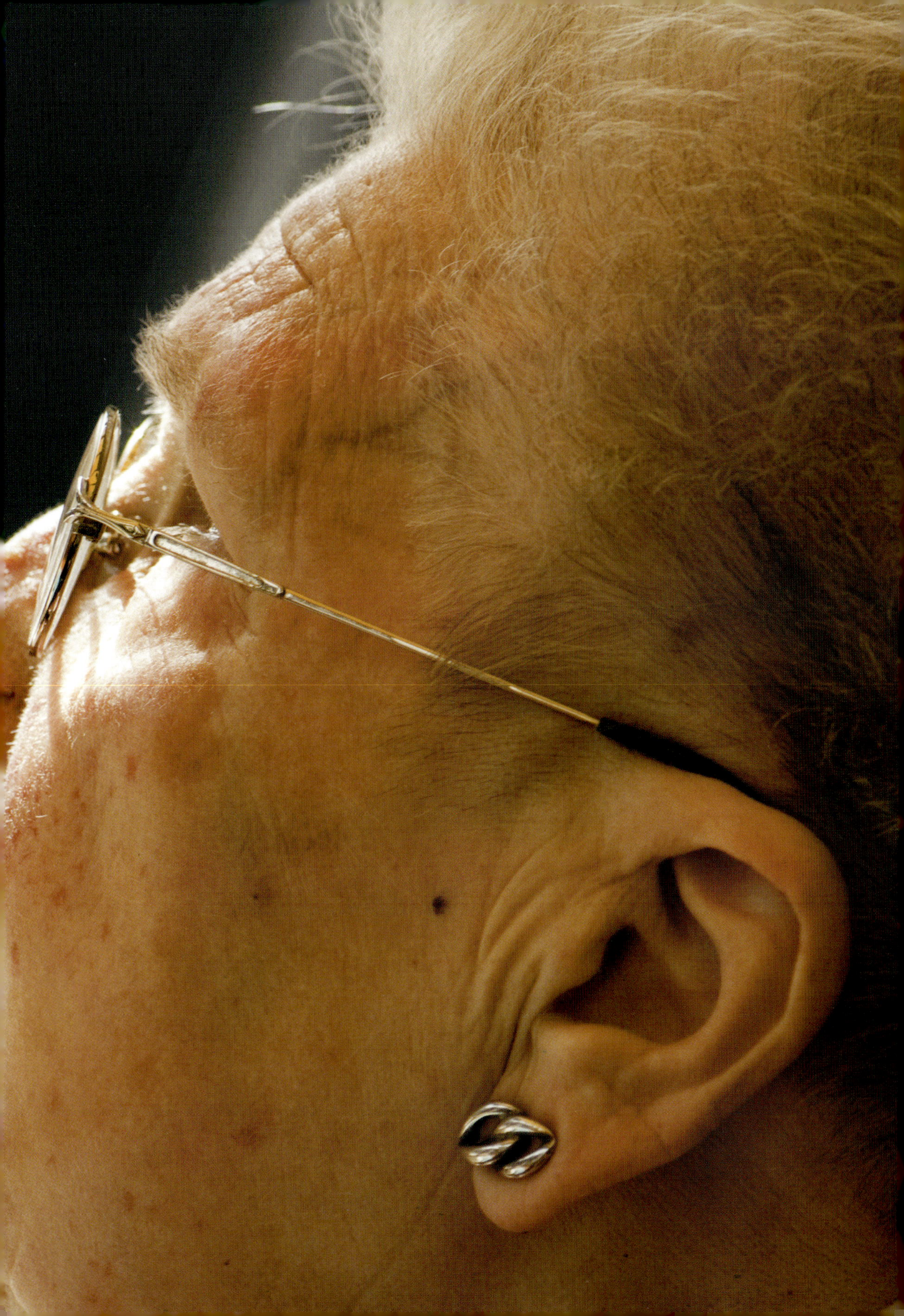

THE PROS AND CONS OF SIZABLE AND MODEST FACILITIES

There are a number of advantages for setting up a reminiscence museum in a sizable facility. In the first place there is, as we stated earlier, the advantage of available space. A reminiscence museum where so many items are stored swallows a huge amount of cubic metres. Large facilities, sometimes many decades old and built in a time when logistic science was still in its infancy, will often contain spacious, vaulted basement areas. Partly empty, or filled with superfluous rubbish to be thrown out anyway. These spaces are perfect for use as a reminiscence museum. Often built over more than forty years ago, they already breathe an air of antiquity. Sizable complexes often come with large lobbies, vast dining rooms and recreational areas, as well as many wide and gloomy corridors. All of them may be brought back to life with museum objects, and together they build up an improvised reminiscence museum.
Sizable facilities, therefore, are excellent to house a museum. Wheel chairs

Mr. Jansen, a nursing home patient for the last 25 years, is still going strong and is seen here having a good time at the reminiscence museum, hospital bed and all. There is room enough for him in the Humanitas basement museum. A smaller building complex would mean that for him to get about would be difficult, a corridor museum would be the answer

Wheelchairs require broad hallways, wide doors, and sufficient room for a wheelchair to make a turn, as is shown here at the museum entrance. Larger complexes have the advantage of such wide corridors and hallways over smaller buildings

require wider pathways, wider doors and room to turn. Humanitas even has clients who visit the museum, bed and all. Another consideration is the necessary storage space for the museum itself. However welcome donations may be, a weekly bulk of half a cubic metre needs to be stored somewhere, before being sorted and distributed. Even the sorting process needs room, which is usually not a problem in larger facilities.

But large organisations offer more than space alone. Often they already have a well-functioning reception area with adequate security equipment which, without extra costs, could also be applied to service the museum. An in-house maintenance service, already present, can help with the construction (put up a dated marble fireplace, place a terrazzo kitchen sink, and construct a wooden partition wall). The already available sizable workshop will accommodate even the larger objects for restoration. These kinds of sizable institutions will also allow the possibility – having the space and the money available - to create a combination of additional happiness-giving matters. Thus Humanitas created, adjacent to the

museum area, a "a fitnessroom" with whirlpools, saunas etc. The light-therapy room, as well as the solarium, are situated in a beach-styled area, which combines a painted background and real objects such as the old-fashioned wicker beach chair and handcart as part of the scenery. Knitted bathing suits and fishing tackle of former days are complementing the beach-scene. As we have stated earlier, reminiscence museums and restaurants are a good match, the latter in keeping with the era, accentuated by style and menu. These restaurants will ensure that a day's outing to the reminiscence museum can be rounded off with a pleasant lunch to make the party a complete success.
Sizable institutions with a large number of employees, volunteer workers, and clients are bound to create a wide support group for a museum. The support is given in manpower, publicity and objects and the museum is sure to be filled with visitors at all times. These kind of activities, again, have a magnet-function for other groups, celebrations, or jubilees.

Still, modestly sized institutions have their advantages, too, for a museum set up. The sense of "this is our museum" will grow much faster and more intense in a smaller institution. Staff and volunteer workers, willing

A Morrocon diningroom is part of the multi-ethical Bergweg museum

to pull their weight, are also much easier to be found. Management, too, being less layered and complicated, will warm more easily to the idea of setting up a reminiscence museum. Besides, modestly sized institutions are more often found in smaller communities, where the local pride in their history is very much alive, and other amusement is hard to find. It will turn the museum into something special, supported by the whole village. This kind of museum can more easily be inspired by the characteristics of the surroundings. A village, historically known as a fishery community, might accentuate the tools and fishing tackle, so characteristic for working and living in a fishery community. The same will hold for an agricultural village, or a coastal resort with its various aspects of life at the beach.

In the smaller care centres, where management often boils down to one person, more support will be found to, for instance, combine a museum visit with a special menu, prepared by the cook, with old-fashioned local dishes which nowadays seem to have disappeared from sight. Presenting a meal of these outdated, nearly forgotten dishes will be the icing on the cake of the birthday-boy, or -girl at their hundredth birthday party. They will bring excitement and conversation topics to the party, so often lacking when the host of the party has become frail, forgetful and less talkative with age.

Local experts are more often inclined to share their expertise voluntarily with a reminiscence museum of a rural, environment-friendly care centre. Sometimes these kinds of localized museums will be realized with the help of existing historical societies. However, please bear in mind that there is a substantial difference with a historical museum, focussed primarily on the conservation, and the long-term historical value, and unique aspect of the objects. On the other hand the reminiscence museum, serving as a community museum as well, is focussed on every-day household objects which almost every visitor will remember from experience or use, and, because everybody remembers them, will create a common ground to generate a feeling of happiness.

Braised meat

Periwinkles

Fried herring

Cows' udder

Fried black pudding

Chapter 10

Economic aspects of a reminiscence museum

Show cases (at about €800 a piece) with museum objects may be placed in hallways and recreational areas already present, as shown here in the Humanitas Akropolis hallway show case, with a display of items from the seventies

Economic aspects of a reminiscence museum

A reminiscence museum, as with every business enterprise, has various financial-economic aspects to be taken into consideration. In the first place, the set-up of a museum will require money. Extensive reconstructions will undoubtedly set you back a few hundred thousand euros. Even when using the already available space, like entrance halls and corridors, and using show cases to display a collection, one still needs to invest in the acquisition of those showcases. In Holland they would cost around €800,- a piece. A relatively small investment, funding of which might well come from national, or local community grants, subsidies, or other funds. And the clients' grateful families might be pleased to be able to make a donation to the cause. Initially, the care organization will also need to purchase objects for a basic collection. To keep costs to a minimum, the immediate circle of family and friends, employees, volunteers and clients need to be made aware of the fact that a museum is in the making. Often the family of a deceased client are loath to throw away, or sell for a pittance, grandfather's old radio, his identity papers from the war, or the old bicycle he used to ride for fifty years. But to donate those items to a reminiscence museum for the benefit and enjoyment of others who are still alive, is another matter entirely. People often welcome the possibility to give meaningful purpose to those inherited objects which were so precious and held emotional value. The organizers of the museum need to be prudent, however, in asking for expensive objects. Simple goods, of little or no value, but so precious to the visitors of the museum, like old sugar bags, or stamps, a gas coin, or dog tag, a bicycle identification tag, or an old tracing-wheel, or maybe a first-issue plastic carrier bag from a well-known store will do more to ignite the excitement and happiness than the sight of an antique, turn-of-the century cabinet. Usually, after an initial modest gift, visitors tend to donate more substantially at a later stage. The proceeds are made up from several different elements. When the museum has a positive effect and improves the reputation of the care institution in such a way, that clients and personnel are easy to come by, it will reduce advertising costs substantially. Furthermore, when such a positive effect of the museum to the organization will be beneficial for employment fall-out, and keeps sick-leave at bay, you have hit the jackpot. When having a museum could be instrumental in enabling the traditional, old-fashioned care institutions to upgrade their image to attract more clients, and prevent vacancies, it could solve their financial problems, and in some cases even ward off

Regularly Humanitas receives museum gifts, in this old ballot box

bankruptcy. Another (financial) advantage may be found in the fact that a regular visit to the museum will diminish the energy-usurping (and therefore costly) tendency some elderly clients have for plaintive behaviour. Sometimes, it might even be possible to prevent rather labour-intensive (and expensive) depressions, merely by the pleasant and activating effect of a museum visit. Humanitas receives financial donations, for the museum regularly. Legacies, although not yet received, are certainly within the realm of possibilities. The turnovers of the bar and restaurant are going up because of the visitors to the museum. The first Humanitas museum attracts about eight thousand external visitors every year. As a result the restaurants have not only cut back on their losses, but are even beginning to turn a profit. In the case of Humanitas it has been established that a number of the cost-saving care volunteer workers have applied for a job, solely from being introduced to the museum. The family is visiting more frequently, too, lured by the happy ambiance which helps grandmother to be less depressed and in the mean time are lending a hand. It is unfortunate that the

In 1918 the Dutch army had to use bicycles with wooden wheels

reminiscence museums have not yet been included in the quality requirements for care institutions in the Netherlands. Clearly this is an omission. More than anything, the reminiscence museum is guaranteed to contribute to the feeling of well-being for the client (and not just for the client). If expenditures and revenues are set off against each other the figures show that the expenditures are mostly of the once-only kind, well within reason, and manageable, and are generating more profits, though not directly measurable in cash, as would appear at first sight. The blueprint budget calculation on page 136 will give a first impression of the financial picture. The deficit on the exploitation side of the budget (summary) could increase with a few thousand euros when writing off the costs of reconstruction, show cases, etc., as well as the costs for electricity, but at the same time be decreased by the lucrative group arrangements in the bar and restaurant, and additional requests for funding, legacies or donations.

Blue print budget calculation for a reminiscence museum.

Expenditures	
Human resources	
Volunteer workers' compensations, Thank-you dinner vouchers, etc.	€ 10.000
Annual purchase of objects	10.000
write-off renovations and equipment	10.000
Cleaning	p.m.[1])
Energy, lighting etc.	p.m.[2])
Telephone, administration,	p.m.[3])
postage etc.	1.000
	€ 31.000

Revenues	
Donations and contributions "Friends of the Museum Foundation"	€ 13.000
Funding and grants	10.000
Sale booklets	p.m.[5])
Sale superfluous items to other reminiscence museums	p.m.[6])
Contributions for group excursions	p.m.
Deficit, taken care of by receipt of legacies, and internal transfer of restaurant profits, or small entrance fees [4]).	8.000
	€ 31.000

1. In the case of Humanitas this item is incorporated in the general maintenance of the building
2. By volunteer workers, or in-house cleaning personnel
3. Item usually incorporated in general expenditures, and is not substantial.
4. An entrance fee might be optional to cut costs. Humanitas provides an old ballot box for voluntary donations.
5. Humanitas nowadays generates a small profit from the sale of documentary booklets.
6. Only to be realized when more reminiscence museums are available, and should be seen in relation to the expenditure item "annual purchase of objects". Occasionally a visitor may wish to purchase an object, provided Humanitas has it in ample supply.

The board of directors giving 'fines' (restaurant vouchers) to the visitors including the police, whom they borrowed their uniforms from

Chapter 11

Outcome of observations, life stories and entries from the guestbook

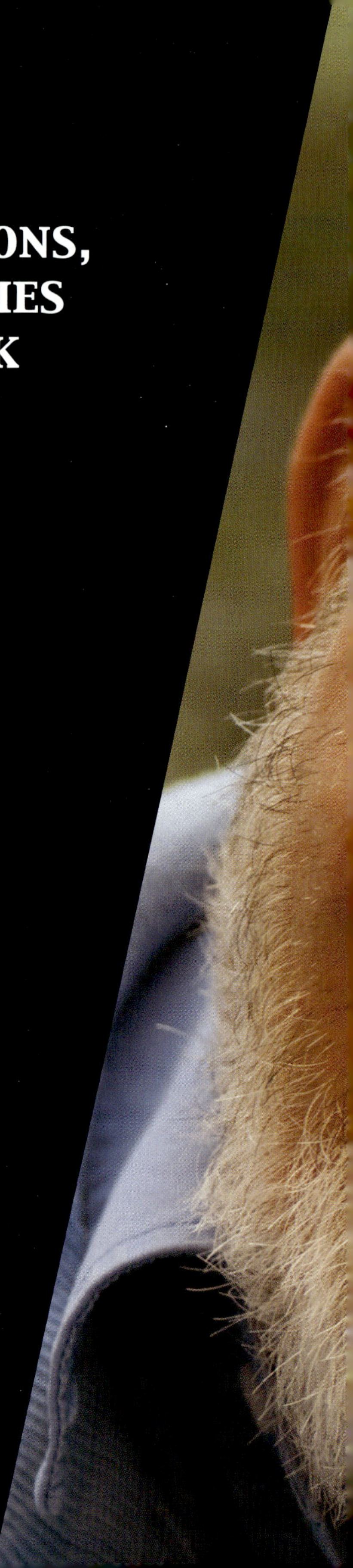

The museum received a gift of a "mourning painting", the weeping willows and gravestone painted with glue and covered with finely chopped hair of the diseased. How we found out? An experiential expert came to visit and told us

OUTCOME OF OBSERVATIONS, LIFE STORIES AND ENTRIES FROM THE GUESTBOOK

We had a hard time determining the origin of a number of objects, which came into possession of the museum. Googling, frequent visits to other museums, as well as intensive research in old books, catalogues and old magazines were at times fruitful, but sometimes we came up with nothing. Substantial sources of information proved to be the visitors themselves: the old fireman of the coal engine locomotive, the midwife, and the farmer's wife from the North county. They often surprised us by explaining the origin and meaning of certain objects. Which were at times most peculiar. As in the instance when the museum obtained an object, later defined as a "mourning painting", the weeping willows and gravestone painted in glue, which were then sprinkled with finely chopped hair of the deceased. A large pair of pliers turned out to be used for curling the zinc on a roof , a small weird-looking wooden reel appeared to have been used for lifting rope-bound paper parcels, a predecessor of the handles of a plastic bag, so to speak. An odd scissoring object was determined by a visitor to be used as a cherry-pip remover from the twenties. A larger-than-life coal shovel with a very short handle appeared to have come from the coal engine of a steam locomotive. Later, as another story pointed out, these shovels were prohibited for safety reasons. A large wooden pair of pincers turned out to be a thistle remover, as an old road worker pointed out. A strange-looking old wooden hollow scoop, as it turned out, was used for bailing water from a flat-bottom boat. In these instances on-the-spot research had taken place spontaneously, with a great allowance for self-esteem, enjoyment and happiness. Many of those painstakingly crocheted bed covers from the parental bedrooms of the thirties, as we were told by visitors, appeared not to have survived the dire circumstances of the Second World War, having been unpicked and re-used for knitting socks. One never stops learning at the reminis-

cence museum. Just as remarkable was the unfamiliarity of urban visitors with many rural objects from the past. Many townspeople would have heard the words flail and hackle during their eighty, or ninety years of life, but had never set eyes on them. Here, not the recognition of the object was of importance, but recollection of the name, for instance from the Bible, or a proverb of old. The baize skirt, well known in our country for featuring in a famous evergreen from the fifties, has also found its niche in the museum. And to be able to finally, after al this time, see and touch the real object provides a new experience, and enjoyment. Something to talk about later and thereby using it to extend one's social network. Observations at the reminiscence museum have shown that the impressions from visitors are in general extremely positive. However, during the nine-months' observation pe-

A large hollow scoop turned out to be used for bailing water from a flat bottom boat

riod some visitors were known to refuse to enter the theme-rooms. Due, it seemed, to some connection with traumatic experiences from the past. As in the example of the old lady who stopped dead at the entrance and refused to move. Only after some gentle coaching by her daughter, herself a volunteer worker at the museum, did she dare set foot in the place. It did not seem to invoke any reaction. We have learned from her daughter that the ensuing flood of memories came later, when they got home. Traumatic experiences from the past resulted in the repression of all childhood memories, including all relevant memorabilia, for decades. In the end the experience had a positive outcome. Being able to share her traumatic experiences had obviously been a relief to her, a feeling she would not have had but for her museum visit.

Another example concerns a nursing home resident, who, almost immediately after entering the museum, said that it was all just old rubbish and she did not care to look at it, anyway. Whether her reaction had been provoked by memories of the past, or her present situation of dependency (she "shares" `her living arrangements in a nursing home with others, does not function independently, and has no possessions of her own anymore) could not be established.

Many city people would have heard about a flail or hackle during their eighty or ninety year lifetime, but had never before set eyes on them

A century-old Dutch custom, where young girls used to have a poem, or verse album, and friends and family were asked to contribute a verse or good wish, to remember them by. Some albums are therefore very rare, and all are endearing and bring forth many memories

These are examples of how visitors' experiences in the museum will involuntarily invoke more than just fun and relaxation. Which does not take away from the fact that a museum visit and its ambiance is mainly meant to be enjoyable, with no strings attached. Given that the museum might clearly have therapeutic value, it may be evident that it is not, first and foremost, meant to be a means of therapy. Reactions are, therefore, spontaneous and involuntary and not provoked for therapeutic purposes. They do, however, provide an excellent opportunity to look for synergies in the communication with the elderly who have difficulties communicating. If a dementia patient has a noticeable reaction on hearing songs of the past, family members, other visitors, and Humanitas staff could take this into consideration and use it to make her museum visit more enjoyable. Browsing through an old photo- or verse album could also serve to enhance enjoyment.

Not long after the opening of the reminiscence museum, students of the Academy of The Hague, carried out a "quick scan" among the visitors. Over a period of twelve days they interviewed 100 visitors. The scan showed that 55 % of the visitors were not Humanitas residents. Ten percent of the respondents had never visited a museum before. The ages of accompanying family members varied between 18 and 80, the majority of which was over 65 years of age. Of these family members 80 % (besides accompanying the elderly) would be inclined to revisit the museum.

Some examples of incidents and anecdotes recorded at the museum are proof how extremely emotional a museum visit might turn out to be. One visitor suddenly removed his shoes to, apparently, once more walk barefoot on the rough sisal carpet from the sixties, a carpet he remembered from his childhood bedroom floor. Another elderly gentleman stood in the grocery-store looking at a Paul Kaiser biscuits tin, moved to tears. The volunteer attendant asked him why he was so upset. It turned out that he had been the former managing director of the firm which bore his name, but that he did not possess a single item at home to remind him of the fact. A lady pointed at the large

Mr. Kaiser, former owner of Kaiser Biscuit factory, was moved to tears at the sight of this tin. At home he had nothing left to remind him of the past and it brought back a flood of memories

floor scales in the shop and recounted how she had to stand on them regularly as a little girl. When asked why, she answered that many children from Rotterdam were undernourished during the war. She was one of them. To get her health back she had been sent to a farm in the Northern part of the country, where she was put on the scales weekly to see if she had gained weight. Despite the fact that these were memories of rather sad times during the war, the story did not seem to make her unhappy. She seemed glad to be able to talk about it and was rather surprised , when triggered by the museum object, to be able to remember so many details from that period in her life.

Most memories are personal, autobiographical by nature. Many visitors will accompany their recollections with more general information about society during a particular period of time. For instance about how the milkman used to simply leave the bottles of milk at the doorstep of one's house. Or how a piece of rope could be seen hanging from the letterbox in the front-door, so that anyone could unlatch the front-door from outside. Then there is the popular story about Monday, laundry day, when hot water was fetched from the 'waterstoker', and drying laundry could be seen hanging along the whole street. Or how the front windows of a house of a recently deceased would be blinded by sheets (their next-door neighbours would do the same) to indicate that a death had occurred. After the funeral the neighbours' blinds were removed, but would be left hanging at the house of the deceased for a while longer.

The guestbook is an important source of information. It records the advice, information, short recollections, or even a first emotional response to someone's encounter with a long forgotten object.

Malnourished children, during wartime "vacations", were put on large scales like these, to see if they had gained weight

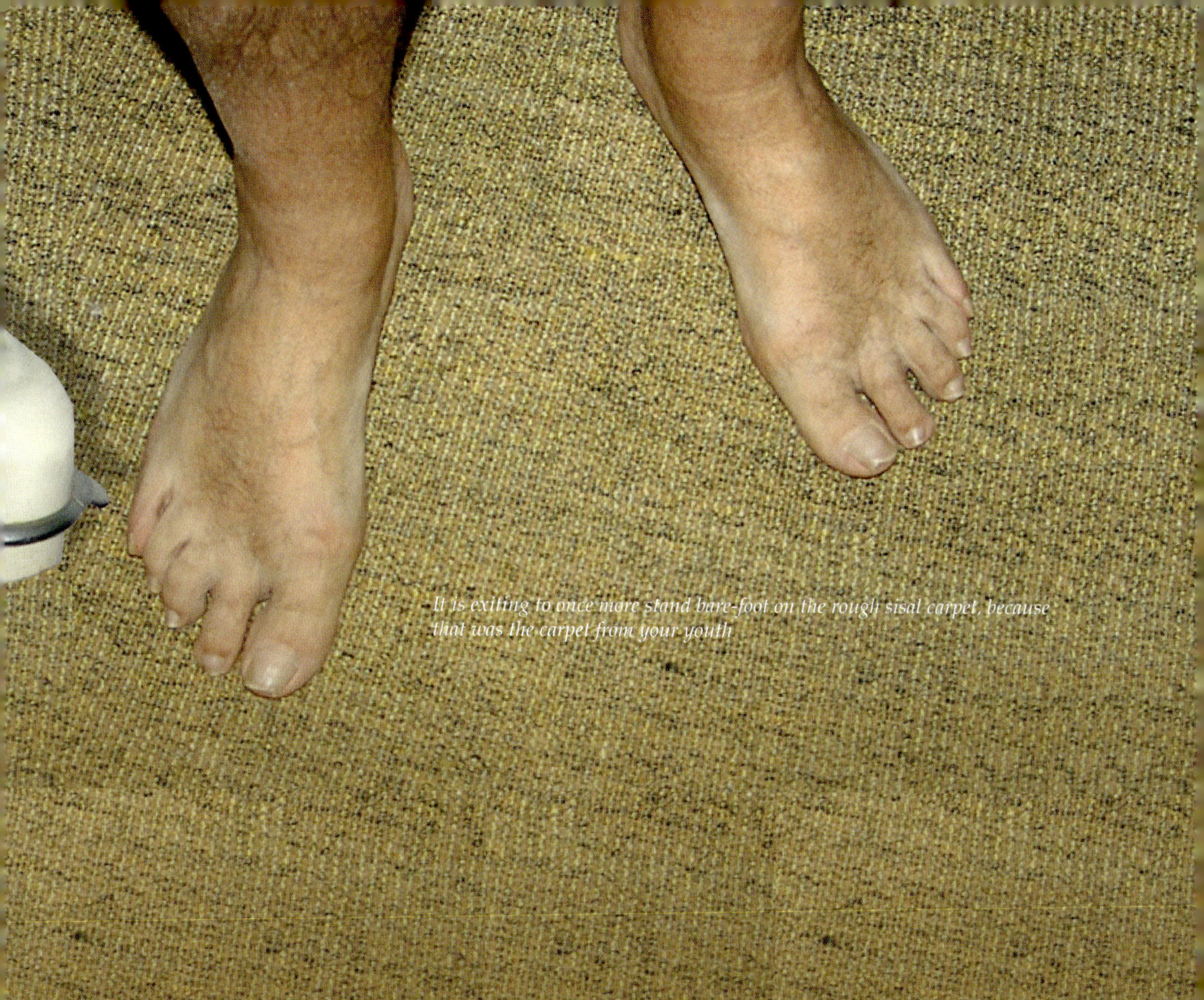

It is exiting to once more stand bare-foot on the rough sisal carpet, because that was the carpet from your youth

Given the fact that a guestbook provides an outlet for responses and possible immaterial contributions, it is of great importance that a guestbook has a prominent place in a reminiscence museum, for visitors to write down their emotions. It is perfect for self-reflection, for the detection of possible improvements, for research on the impact of a museum visit on visitors, and for encouragement.

As we have stated before, the majority of the museum visits are carried out with a positive spirit and are greatly appreciated. A number of things did catch our attention, though: the visitors' surprise at the sheer volume of the exhibition, how easy it was for memories to come back when triggered, and the pride and gratitude for the opportunity to assist in the creation of the collection (and later to see and point out their own donations) and give their comments.

The memories and the possibility to recognize one's own experiences in the recollections of others, will create a rather special atmosphere of trust

State Secretary of Public Health, Jet Bussemaker, wrote in the reminiscence museum guestbook in March 2008: A wonderful museum of surprise, recognition and wonder. Really very beautiful, and part of a splendid Humanitas concept

between visitors. And it is catching. Almost every visit becomes a positively charged experience, to be remembered and talked about for a long time. And interactions like these will create an extension of social network and diminish loneliness. Which creates new life force and, whilst preparing for a follow-up visit, the positive effects of the experience will remain.

The museum, therefore, is offering a variety of multi-sensory stimuli. These stimuli are divers in effectiveness, depending on the individual abilities and experiences of visitors. Measured by the responses of people, smell, sound and touch are the most successful stimuli, even more so than sight. Listening to fragments of old radio programs is often the most amusing moment of the visit. And its power lies not only in the individual recognition, but in the interactive nature of the experience. People join in sing-along tunes, move to the rhythm of the music and even join in the exercises when listening to an early morning workout program of fifty years ago. The reactions to the smell of moth balls or cod liver oil are amazing: first there is the recognition, then comes the commentary on the unpleasant smell or taste and after that follows an interchange of anecdotes. Visitors who recognize a "Buisman" (Dutch brand of chicory) tin are inclined to open it. And finding the tin still filled and giving off its unmistakable smell will ensue in a flood of memories.

Which means that there is enough reason to take this into consideration when designing the lay-out of the museum: the more complex and circumstantial the stimuli are presented, the more influence and effect it will have on the visitors. The visitors need to be goaded into curiosity, so to speak, and be made to investigate for themselves. The outcome will be much more powerful than, for instance, the volunteer attendant giving a standardized performance of opening a Buisman tin. To peruse through the museum, with a list of rather unfamiliar items at hand, is therefore such fun to do.

Gender-wise, not surprisingly, there is a marked difference in the reactions of men and women. Women are more apt to determine the origins of household objects. They are obviously more dominant in the sewing room and kitchen. The shed and photography department are, however, largely male territory, when reminiscing about handiwork and hobby's, and the same applies for the displayed motorbikes and scooters. The gentleman's study with the gramophone player, travelling guides, financial memorabilia, the cigars and the old typewriter, too, will evoke more comments from men than women. In the exceptional cases where the tables are turned, anecdotes and observations will soon reveal the reasons why.

The smells and scents the reminiscence museum tried to conjure up held and unexpected surprise for us in store. The artificially constructed smells Humanitas had purchased were not satisfactory. In the first place only a limited range of smells were available, and these were of a poor quality as well. The solution was simply to recreate forgotten smells in the usual way, such as producing a genuine soapsud-smell with real soap, using real chopped leeks, sprinkle some petrol around on the floor (petrol has been a long-standing remedy for lice), keep some tar warm on an electrical stove, discreetly hidden at the back of the room, and some real beeswax and linseed oil on the displayed furniture. To have an old, still usable, washing machine churning away in a corner proved to give off a very effective smelling sensation. Just leave a cod liver oil bottle uncorked so people can pick it up and smell it. An excellent way to create a pleasant kitchen smell is to fry a little bacon on the stove. In the shop the onions and leeks need to be refreshed regularly to create an effective shop aroma with little cost and effort.

In the audio-visual department, the experiment to transform a television set from the sixties into a set where, by using a DVD, it is possible to show old programs in black and white from the past, proved to be highly successful. The movie "Fanfare" ("Brass Band") by Dutch film director Bert Haanstra, for instance, is thus shown on screen with some kind of authenticity. The modified radio, with pilot eye, broadcasting tunes and football results from the fifties, followed by a once very popular morning workout program, as well as the "sewing class" program of old, have been an excellent way to bring back memories.

It is interesting to observe how on the reading table in the library, or reception hall, some worn ladies' magazines from the sixties are peacefully fraternizing with monthly pediodicals from the thirties, and historical publications from the twenties, which are very much sought after. It appears to be a pleasant pastime for visitors who are interested in reading up on the publications of other times, and share their memories with fellow-readers around the table. Well documented reports with some awesome illustrations on, for instance, the great flood of 1953, the wedding of Queen Juliana, and the terrors of the Second World War, will assist to bring back memories in a rather confronting manner. Such a reading table, however, ought to be part of the ambiance of the museum, meaning that the use of superfluous institution furniture, however indestructible, is out of the question.

There are a few things worth considering with regards to the nursing home mentally challenged patients (a visiting partner once described the situation as "her thoughts are failing her"). In the first place it is imperative to take the necessary time. The museum visit should not be a rush-job. It might be wise to set a time-limit. Often it is enough to visit a few sections at a time, to avoid too many impressions crowding the minds of people with limited perception and communication skills. Also, a great deal of patience is required from the attending volunteer guides. Waiting for an answer may take some time. Still, it is important to have one's question

Vegetables need to be refreshed regularly to create a grocery store aroma. It looks good, too. Onions, potatoes and apples will store well for a long time. Visitors seem to appreciate the sight of these real vegetables

answered. The right positioning of the body, combined with some communication skills are, therefore, the first requirements. Which implies that shouting into a clients' ear from behind the wheelchair, while being invisible to the client, is counter-productive. Position yourself in front of the client, kneeling down or sitting down on a bench, and make eye contact. Even more so than with non-dementia elderly visitors, it is important to search for those objects, sounds, smells and visual material, which might evoke a reaction. It might be helpful for the volunteer guide to inquire about the visitor's background at the start of the tour. Furthermore, it is essential to advise visitors that touching and handling the objects such as small stools, bicycles and chairs is perfectly allowed and that one is free to join in at the regulars' table to play a game of Ludo.

With the exception, perhaps, where large groups of visitors are concerned, generally speaking the attending volunteer guides ought to be instructed on how to improve their questioning skills. "Do you know what this is?, What was it like in your time?, Did you ever use those tools?" rather than relating stories themselves. It may be difficult at times as many attendants like to guide their visitors the way it is done in regular museums, namely by doing the explaining themselves. It is a completely different situation with a reminiscence museum. Showing a genuine interest in the visitors' backgrounds and asking open questions, which may cause them to tap into whatever is still stored in their minds, is considered a primary task for the volunteer attendant. To be a good volunteer guide, it is important to learn the difference between a question like "How did you take your bath when you were young?", and "Did you also have a bath in a sink tub in the kitchen?"

Recalling smells from olden days by, for instance, spilling a little petrol on the floor is not hard to do and has a marked effect on visitors

Chapter 12

Possible inconsistencies

The educational element is a mere by-product, but is enhanced by touching and handling of objects and the ensuing informative conversations

POSSIBLE INCONSISTENCIES

The question of some possible inconsistencies might arise, which will be addressed here. Does the set-up of the reminiscence museum have a negative effect on the conservation of objects? Will the objects not be unduly damaged when handled by the visitors? In the absence of professional attendants and with the freedom to handle and move objects, how about theft and security?

Of course these are valid observations, but bearing in mind that these common and every-day household objects from the past are not expensive, and take preference over the valuable one-of-a- kind objects, some breakage and loss is within the scope of things (though preferably not). Moreover, the display of objects in a reminiscence museum usually covers items which were made to last and are generally not very appealing to be taken home anyway. And, given the age of the mostly elderly visiting public, they are generally more careful and less inclined to vandalise, or steal. Quite the opposite: they often offer to restore or supply spare parts for any damaged items, sometimes even coming back with a better specimen of the object already on display.

Will the pleasant gatherings, intentionally kept frivolous, not infringe on the educational and research values of the project? Certainly not. In the first place education is not the primary objective of the reminiscence museum, but even as a secundary objective, the educational value is enhanced by the enjoyment of handling the objects and the ensuing conversations. Call it a kind of serendipity. (the effect of creating something positive unintentionally, while searching for something completely different; sometimes also created when "making virtue out of necessity"). Besides which the stories of what is uniquely stored in the mind of the visitor will provide ample opportunity for research.

Does the sheer volume of the display not stand in the way of a relaxed browsing through one's memories? This observation certainly validates the attention of the organization. A museum visit should not degenera-

The thematic display evokes an atmosphere to induce memories of a certain era, and facilitates reminiscence possibilities. Displays of collections of similar individual objects are the threads which trigger the memories. Both varieties are compatible

te into a tiresome journey through what looks like a junk-shop or flea-market. An overdose of impressions, for instance with dementia patients, might easily occur. On the one hand, the elderly generally do not have the stamina to take in a multitude of impressions for a longer period of time. On the other hand, one needs to bear in mind that the elderly have time to spare and are usually living within the walls of the care organization, or in the vicinity, and the (free) visits to the reminiscence museum are well within their scope.

The specific lay-out of the reminiscence museum might also prevent an overdose of impressions. The thematic display will create a certain atmosphere. An atmosphere to stimulate recollections of the past, inducing the possibility to reminisce. Nobel Prize winner Professor Eric Kandel expressed it as learning things by association because they happen in specific surroundings. The characteristics of those surroundings, the particular lighting, the other people present, the smells, are such associations. When bringing back a memory, one piece of thread of these particular associations is pulled. All senses are, by themselves, capable of triggering certain memories.

The elderly have impaired mobility, are relying on walking frames and electric wheelchairs. Sometimes they have very little energy left, which makes it imperative for the museum to be close by, and within easy reach

A collection of electric heaters, a few of which are shown here, demonstrates the diversity of heating facilities available, in the time before central heating was invented. The donated collection of hot water bottles and foot-warmers gives a similar impression. Both will evoke memories from the time when people were really suffering from the cold

The extensive collection of similar objects in the show cases will enable a search for – and find - precisely the sugar bowl which you owned yourself, and to centre one's memories on the object. Visitors, therefore, have a choice on how to use the museum lay-out: breathe in the atmosphere of an era, or look for specific objects like the ones they once owned. Either way, it may be experienced simultaneously, or in succession.

The question may rise whether the set up of a chain of reminiscence museums, as Humanitas intends to do, might not be too much of a good thing, and whether this would have any additional value. A number of points should be taken into consideration :

- The reminiscence museum is primarily targeting an elderly public. A clientele whose mobility often has decreased significantly, relying on walking frames and scoot mobiles to get about. They also have a limited supply of energy. And it is so important for these elderly not to have to depend on made-to-measure transport buses to hoist them back and forth, electric wheelchair included. In order to enjoy a thirty minute visit to the museum, the museum should be within close proximity. Which means in reality that every care institution ought to have a facility like this, if only for the opportunity to just nip over for a visit with one's relatives.

- Another consideration is that – even with a similar set-up – the location and lay-out may differ for every museum. A museum integrated in the restaurant, or boardroom, differs considerably from a ribbon-like museum through endless corridors . A basement museum again, has a completely different outlook.
- A specific museum collection, accumulated further by gifts and donations, will grow rather randomly. It even accumulates without the need for a complete collection. Owing to the lack of budget to purchase specific objects, one depends to a large extent on what is donated, but therein lies the fun.
- Humanitas has noticed that the kinds of donations combined with a specific lay-out have created a great variety and individuality and each reminiscence museum eventually has evolved its own specific character. They are, after all, real community museums.

As stated above, the variety of museum characteristics will evolve more or less randomly. Which is a good thing. The past, after all, is "une mer a boire" ("a sea to drink") from, so extensive, one should not even attempt to capture the complete picture. The largest Humanitas reminiscence museum covers about 400 m2 , divided over 14 sections. This may seem large, but in relation to the vast quantities of reminiscence objects available, it is rather limited. When private collectors, or their heirs, donate a collection of sewing machines to the museum, it gives a different emphasis on the lay-out of the display, than a collection of matchboxes might, or tins. However, there is no rule against accentuating an existing theme even further by trying to obtain more of the same on e-Bay, for instance. When one is presented with a handsome collection of hot water bottles and footwarmers, as happened to Humanitas, it resulted in the collection of a range of electric heaters as well, to show the variety of ways heating was accomplished in a time when central heating was not commom.
A final possible inconsistency might be found in the static character every museum seems to have by rights. Will not the visitors get so complacent about the current basic collection, that it will no longer evoke new memories? Luckily there is no fear of that, due to the volume of objects and the constant flow of new acquisitions. There is also the possibility to extend the basic collection with "roadshow" collections. Humanitas has a

few showcases in every museum where, at regular intervals, a circulating theme collection will be shown featuring, for instance, Easter and Christmas. At the same time, Humanitas has circulating theme collections for her museums – nine museums are envisaged for the future - concerning: "royalty", "sports memorabilia from the fifties and sixties", "make do and mend", "terrors of the Second World War", etc. These roadshow collections will make each visit to the museum, which are free and therefore easily accessible for people with limited means, an amazing experience. Besides, the fact remains that the clientele of the care institutions is replaced at a relatively high rate, and with them their family and friends. Statistically, a somatic, care institution indicated elderly person will have died within two-and-a-half years. Automatically it will cause a high exchange-frequency of museum visitors with their circle of families and friends. Admittedly, the elderly usually have elderly acquaintances, and precisely this irregularity and variety of the visiting public, with their different life stories, is the backbone of the ever-changing emphasis of the museum collection.

A Turkisch carpet, like this silk one from Kayseri, is not only famous in Turkey but also in the Netherlands

Chapter 13

The multi-cultural connecting element of the museum

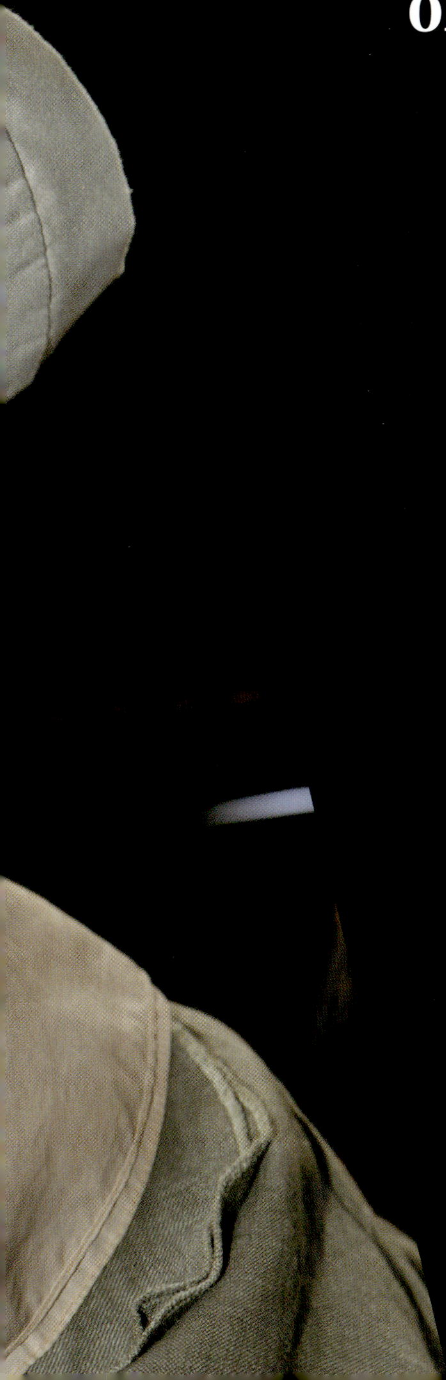

THE MULTI-CULTURAL CONNECTING ELEMENT OF THE MUSEUM

One of the pleasant advantages of a reminiscence museum is that it will bring about some kind of fraternization between people of different ethnic heritage. The fact is that visitors from different ethnic backgrounds will discover here that their roots are similar. Besides which, there is a growing number of people of different ethnicity participating in the elderly care. Humanitas already has as many as 41 different nationalities amongst her personnel.

An impoverished society, as the Netherlands were before, during, and short after the Second World War, has much in common with other impoverished societies. There is a lack of money, therefore: Sunlight soap without a wrapper, Eau de Cologne is refilled as bottles were expensive, there are saving tins for various expenses, like gas coins, etc., meals need to be prepared, even without a gas mains or electricity, so one used wood, petrol or butane gas. One needs to grind the coffee beans, even when electric coffee grinders are not available. And the way this was done was similar in the Netherlands as well as in Turkey. Without running tap-water, water was still a necessity, so there would be a water-well available with a bucket and a rope, or a hand pump. Clothes still needed to be washed, even when there was no electric washing machine. In the home something like a wash tub would have been available. Without tap-water, one would

The leather fire-bucket from a century ago, looks amazingly like the contemporary Moroccan bucket, made from car tires

When there are no water mains, ewers or water jugs could be found in the household, whether it be in Holland or Morocco. The coffee beans needed grinding, even before electric coffee grinders were available, whether it be in the Netherlands or Turkey

Surinam nostalgia

have ewers or jugs in the home, or some other kind of reservoir. Clothes needed to be mended, certainly in times of poverty when they were made to last, and if the tailor or seamstress was too expensive, one needed to have sewing equipment in the home. The same goes for mending shoes, in the absence of a cobbler. Tools to fix things in and around the house were essential, as were the tools for the vegetable patch. Children needed to play, so, lovingly, toys were fabricated from waste material. These things know no borders. The same way that in Holland in the pre-plastics era leather buckets were used by the fire brigade, similarly, buckets were made from old car tires in Morocco for use at the water well. In those times food needed to be transported, so similar-looking stack-and-store pans were used in Holland and Turkey alike, and have proved their worth for decades.

When a century ago, adequate packaging materials were not available yet, in Holland the use of a "sugar-loaf", consisting of compressed sugar, was commonly known and nowadays this is still very much in use in Morocco. Over time, tapping off the sugar lumps with a special sugar hammer has become quite a ritual there. In a poor society, a tea-house with cheap tea, served in small glasses, is a boon and a blessing. Which is why the tea-houses in Morocco, and the old-fashioned tea rooms in Western Europe are commonly rooted.

Making do and mend, as well as the need for survival, are creating the same circumstances everywhere and will reflect in a similar range of objects and rituals. The D.I.Y. activities, born from necessity in the poverty-stricken housing of the time, doing the laundry and scrubbing with a tub and washboard, having a paraffin stove for cooking and a kerosene lamp for lighting, they are all instrumental in obscuring geographical and ethnic boundaries, and create a feeling of fraternization and unity. Whether one needs to move about in the snow in Norway, or in Turkey, there will always be the need for some kind of snow shoes, or skis.

The mutual acknowledgement, even by the now thriving second and third generation of immigrant clients, of similar problem situations which demanded similar solutions in the past, may have a useful connecting function in our multi-ethnic society. It will lower the threshold for

Carribian nostalgia

In the pre-plastics era similar looking stack-and-store pans were used in the Netherlands as well as in Turkey

immigrant clients whom, by being a minority and therefore not yet familiar with the care institution's traditions, will experience such a threshold even more acutely than the native elderly people when moving to a care institution. In this way the reminiscence museum may pave the way to a better understanding of the care institutions and improve their image for immigrant clients.

It is rather fun to observe how first generation Turkish and Moroccan immigrants who, forty years ago, were confronted with the same simple objects as the Dutch, will find themselves in a similar state of enthusiastic recognition in the museum as the elderly Dutch visitors. The coal fire brings back memories of how, in the early immigrant workers' boarding houses, they would gather round the large circular coal fire, the only source of heating at the time, something they had not set eyes on for over forty years. There were other reactions from a group of Moroccan visitors to the museum. Stories of washing clothes on a Moroccan river bank, using a pumice stone and scrubber, the water kettle, and the furnace with butane gas. The old typewriter which, in a largely illiterate society, was used by the "writers" on the market square. And how about the sewing machine: mending was done on the market square by tailors – with Singer and Pfaff sewing machines. The tool shed also contains well-known appliances and tools: the shoe-last, the planes and gouges, the chisels and whetting stones. Not exactly tools from the past for many immigrants. Most tools are still very much in use in today's Turkey and Morocco.

It is rather amusing to observe how young relatives of immigrant clients, on a visit to the museum, are getting interested in the displays. As is the case with native youths, who are usually not in the habit of visiting a museum either, the threshold for visiting a regular museum may thus be lowered. Finding each other on a visit to the cultural heritage, communicating about the differences and similarities, will stimulate fraternization and integration. In many ways it confirms the theory of Sandell that museums have the ability to stimulate tolerance and respect between communities, as well as challenge the existing stereotypes. Which is quite in line with the

The coal fire evokes memories from early immigrants, back to the years (some forty years ago) that they gathered around the large fireplace in their boarding houses - the only source of warmth at the time

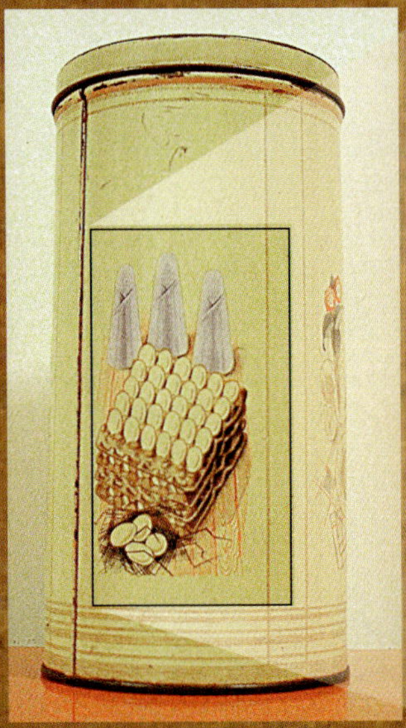

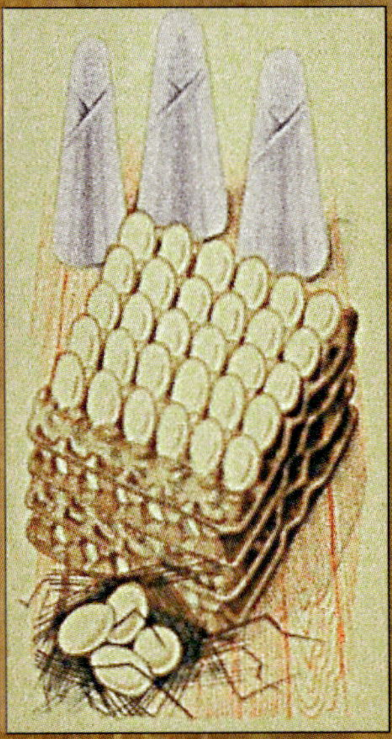

A century ago, the so-called "sugar-loaf", made from compressed sugar in a time when efficient packing material was not available, was familiar in Holland (note the illustration on the tin on photo left) and it is still in use in Morocco (photo right)

theory of Claudine Brown, who poses that accessibility is mandatory: *Every museum should see itself as a neighbourhood museum. If an institution is not accessible to the individuals who must of necessity pass by its portals each day, then it is not a truly public institution.*

Therefore it is a good thing that "passing" visitors from Surinam and the Antilles will be able to recognize the old Singer sewing-machine and Reckitt's Blue whitener, the same way the Dutch visitors will , and so experience the same roots.

Whether one needed to move about in the snow in Norway, or in Turkey, one needed the use of snow-shoes, or skis, as the Turkish ones shown here

Turkish nostalgia

The Dutch Indies, nowadays the Republic of Indonesia , were for almost three and a half century the largest colony of the Netherlands. Consequently the Netherlands were for centuries the largest islamic nation in the world

Chapter 14

The influence of the reminiscence museum on the image of care institutions:

'Temples of vivacious culture and reminiscence' instead of 'Misery-islands as waiting-rooms of death'

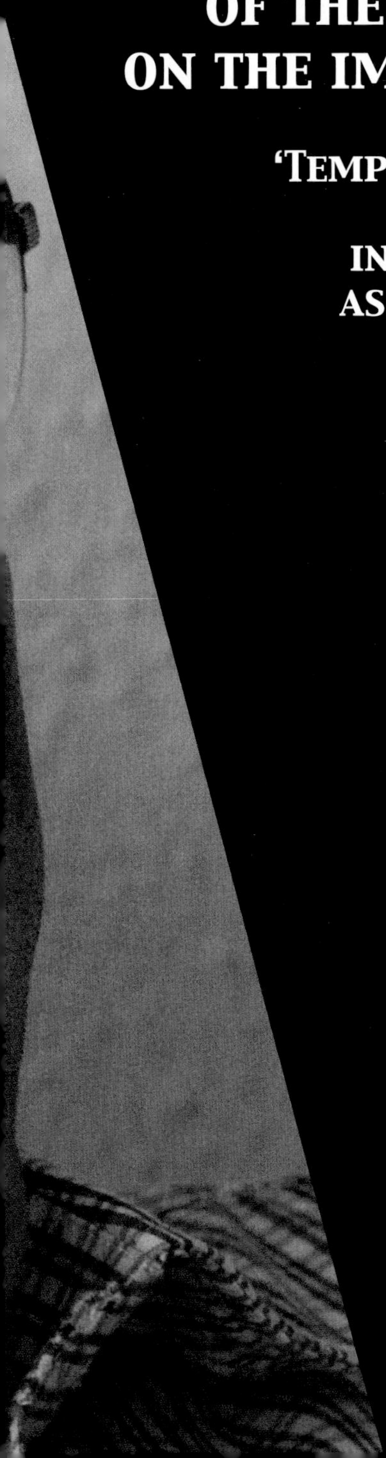

THE INFLUENCE OF THE REMINISCENCE MUSEUM ON THE IMAGE OF CARE INSTITUTIONS:

"TEMPLES OF VIVACIOUS CULTURE AND REMINISCENCE" INSTEAD OF "MISERY-ISLANDS AS WAITING-ROOMS OF DEATH".

An interesting aspect is the way in which reminiscence museums are having an impact on the image of the care organizations. An important image at that, if the organization is to secure new clients and recruit personnel and volunteer workers. In an increasingly ageing society, where structurally more clients are demanding care and, therefore, more care workers are needed, there is a structural need for more personnel to be employed and trained to work in the elderly care. Just as vitally important is attracting more volunteer workers and/or wrap-around care. To have a good image may then be an asset. Which is why the care institutions

It is important to take care of the positive image of care institutions. Aside from the positive contribution provided by the reminiscence museums, other activities need to be exposed to the media often and celebrated lavishly. Shown here Her Majesty The Queen of The Netherlands, who is being presented with a lovely bouquet of flowers by one of the Humanitas residents

A first encounter with the care institution will be made exiting, happy and pleasant on account of the reminiscence museum. Which is also a good boost for the run-down image of the institutions in general

should not let up on their endeavours to improve their image. Jubilees, first posts, and opening ceremonies of brand-new, or beautifully restored buildings with some grandeur (graced by the Queen's presence, attended by ministers, and other celebrities) together with all the clients and their families - celebrate them lavishly, and in style.

Unfortunately, the image of the elderly care leaves a lot to be desired. The continuing and endless bickering over the rather unattractive collective labour agreements, still ongoing economizing and scaling down of budgets, combined with excesses such as "pyjamas-days* " , "restraining measures" and "lavatory-times", are the cause of many youngsters deciding instead to take a job at a jolly camping or a friendly supermarket. And if they do decide to work in health care after all, they prefer to choose one of those high profile hospitals, which are made out to be more interesting and attractive by television soaps. The same goes for volunteer workers, who will think twice before offering their services to a bureaucratic, over-organized would-be hospital, based on a "no-culture", with the slight but unmistakable smell of urine.

Still, working in the elderly care, looking after clients with such diversity of careers and life experiences is, in principle, rather fun and quite rewarding. As long as it is managed in the right way. Humanitas has expressed

** pyjamas days i.e. due to lack of staff, clients remain in their nighties during the day instead of being assisted by dressing*

A famous Dutch singer, Lee Towers giving a heart-warming performance for his resident mother and her peers

her theories on management, which include the reminiscence museum, in her Corporate Story, well outlined in the book "Corporate Stories" (see appendices). The theory behind the reminiscence museums has been excellently worded and richly illustrated in the beautiful book by Herman Moscoviter "Open the shutters of your memory".
The reminiscence museum is a perfect medium to show how much fun elderly care can be. It serves as a connecting element between personnel and clients, clients amongst themselves, and clients with their families. A first introduction to the care institution will, on account of the reminiscence museum objects, immediately become an exiting and happy experience. The ever present medical/hygienic atmosphere will at any rate become less dominant, and the assertiveness, expertise, humour and life experience of the elderly clients will clearly come to life at the museum.
Image building is not only important for the acquisition of personnel and volunteer workers. The right image is instrumental in lowering the threshold for elderly clients who are forced to take the, often so painful, decision to move to a care institution, in whatever capacity that may be. The museum can, by her positive effect on the client and family assisting with the move, improve the accessibility to the new abode, thus reducing the awkwardness of the transition.

Annie de Reuver one of Holland's most famous performers, and with her 93 years a shining example of use it or lose it, is still a very active Humanitas resident

In this day and age where standards, values and identity have been given a new lease on life, the care institutions, by way of the reminiscence museums, may even become the bearers and custodians to hand down our culture. For all knowledge still stored within the minds of clients and visitors need only to be activated by the museum, in order to be

When the buildings are an architect's dream, beautifully designed, with a luxurious and lively atrium, it will undoubtedly boost the image. But with an additional reminiscence museum, the interactions will be intensified, conversation topics will be extensive and varied, and add to the positive memories of a visit to the institution

handed down. It may be recorded by word of mouth, on video tape, but also in writing. A number of recorded life stories and remarks from the guestbook in the appendix will give a general impression.

Given the fact that a somatic, care institution- indicated elderly client will statistically die within a few years, it is this natural flow of museum clientele which, in fact, provides an ongoing renewal of fresh sources of knowledge to be tapped into and recorded. Which, in turn, will have a positive influence on the atmosphere and image. The steady growth of the basic collection will also lead to connecting points for new stories about the way life was lived in the past. The atmosphere and activities tend to be focussed on liveliness, life stories and fun, rather than on the more run-of-the-mill medical/hygienic, hospital-like approach. In this way the reminiscence museum, by building up the corporate identity, will contribute considerably to a change in perception of the workings and image of the care institutions. How these matters are already influencing the media is shown in the appendix "How did the media respond to the first reminiscence museum?"

There are, of course, many more ways to go about image-building. A beautifully designed building (the "upended matchbox" kind are still a regular feature, alas) with a luxurious and lively atrium will be an asset. When the restaurants for the elderly are known for their quality and service, occasionally featuring prominent artists and frequented by politicians (if only because their parents are residents - as in the case of Humanitas, where for instance one of our leading Dutch singers, Annie de Reuver, a resident herself, is still performing regularly), when there are lavish and sparkling parties, a nice animal garden, these assets will certainly be a boost for the elderly care image. The cultural steering itself, with its core values of self-direction, self-assertiveness, belonging to a large extended family, and the "yes"-culture, will undoubtedly be a push in the right direction to improve the image of the elderly care.
But it is, without a doubt, the reminiscence museum itself which provides a fair chance to eliminate the present image of the care institutions, as being misery islands with bad working conditions and ditto payment, and instead create an image of interesting, amusing, lively and exiting "temples of vivacious culture and reminiscence", where the living is good.

APPENDIX

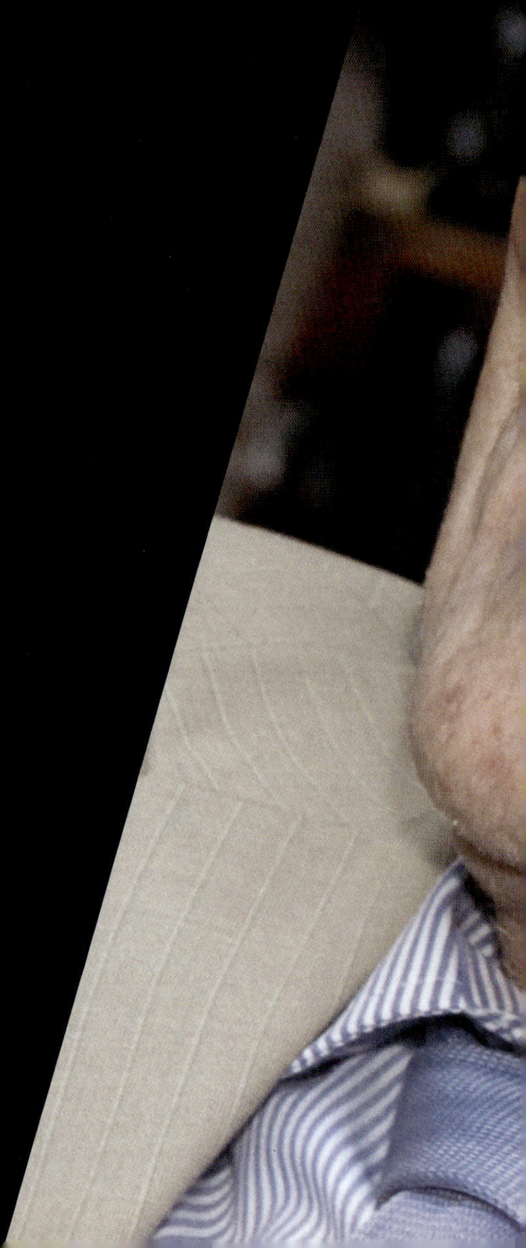

"Harvest" from the guestbook:

A selection from hundreds of reactions.

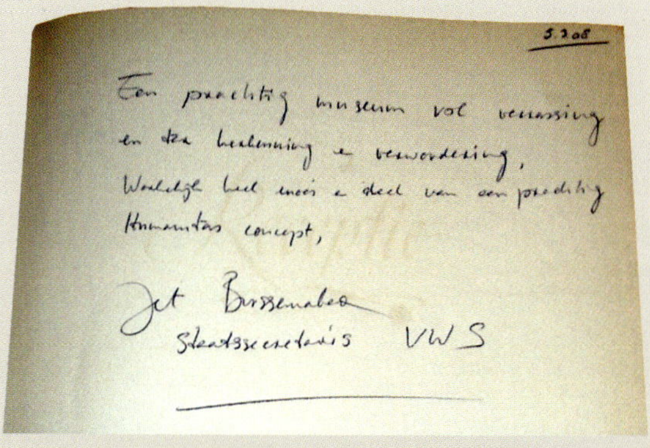

State Secretary of Public Health, Jet Bussemakers, visited the reminiscence museum on March 5th, 2008 and on that occasion made a clear and apt comment in the guestbook that the reminiscence museum is an integral part of the Humanitas concept

"Harvest" from the guestbook, and other reactions.

Very special, this museum, and a real asset for the elderly care. This way they will certainly feel even more at home. Now I know the place to donate my treasures to! Fantastic; never seen anything like it before. So complete.

One Sunday afternoon, we had a visit from a jolly old lady. The fact that she was in a wheel-chair notwithstanding, she was beaming with pleasure and enjoyed all there was to see. When she had seen it all, she spread her arms wide and cried out enthusiastically : "How I wish I could take everything home with me!". Then, obviously taken aback by what she had said, she excused herself softly by saying "Not to own it all, you know, but just because it makes me feel so happy...".

A feast of recognition. My boss's Solex (motorbike) used to be out of bounds for me, but I rode it anyway, secretly. Let's see if I can still ride it now!

It seems as if I am back at my granny's place. Just add a ship in a bottle and it will be my grandpa's house.

Old things, too, can still have their charm and there is a lot to be learned from them. My whole life can be seen here, starting with the towel horse in front of the coal fire, and so on. We have relived our childhood memories. How enjoyable, and if ever I come across some "old rubbish", I'll know it will find a good home here.

A feast of recognition, whether you are 85 or 55! A good thing that so many things have been saved! Very emotional trip down memory lane, and this is such a good way to do that. I hope that this will stay, to return to over and over again and go back in time, many thanks for this. So educational to see all these things again, from days gone by. Educational for the younger generation, too, from an era when things were not taken for granted.

We have been clubmates since 1947, when we were in our first year of high school. Some girls failed the exams that year, and we called ourselves "the left-overs". Later some men joined the club and we went out together. There was a time when we were all busy with our own families, but the friendship remained. Now we are all older and are still trying to go for a twice-yearly outing together. We may be older, but the club "the left-overs" is still going strong. This is a beautiful collection, please look after it well, for the future.

Well, here we are, at Akropolis, Rotterdam. So much atmosphere, I can see myself here, at some time in the future. A beautiful day, and such an enthusiastic tour-guide! Many thanks. Moments of recognition, sweet memories of our youth and parental and grandparental homes, just great!

What was most impressive was the towel-horse in front of the coal heater (and the war-time heaters and stoves). Some remarks from the children. Brian: liked the living room. Marco: liked the swivel chair.

Such fun that you can touch and try out everything in this museum. I have been able to see how my grandmother and grandfather lived in their time, really great.

The lay-out is nice, well thought out economically. This ought to be followed up, other care centres should follow this example.

The residents of Care Centre "Zuijdtwijck" from Leiden, Holland, have so enjoyed seeing all the objects in this museum. They were reminiscing about their childhood. What a super idea! We will certainly be back with more residents.

Awesome, this retrospective view, in our home we do not have anything further back than the sixties. This collection goes back even further, really great! My mother and I have been so surprised, and we marvelled at all the objects of the past. Such a beautiful collection of memories of times gone by - "when happiness used to be a matter of course".

Having seen all this, I had not realized I am this old already! Feast of recognition. This is the first time for me, but it quite opens up your heart. Imagining myself back in time, it was just staggering, For a moment I felt young again!

Came to Holland from Surinam in 1960, and today, May 17th, 2007, when I am 70 years of age, I am looking again at my mother's old Singer sewing machine,

and so many other things we had in our home in Surinam. My mother is now 94 years old. I am so moved to see all these objects from my youth again.

What a pleasant reception by your museum team. The ladies from the conversation club "Back to times gone by" have all enjoyed their visit tremendously. Again! This is our 6th visit already. With other people the recollections are always different and more fun. Well done and keep it up! Very nice volunteer workers!

Many memories came flooding back from the "good old days". Fortunately, nowadays we do not have to do the laundry the way we have seen here. The Ladies Advisory Committee, Geldermalsen.

We have enjoyed seeing so many recognizable objects. With tears in my eyes I have been looking around at all those beautiful things. How good it was in those days, and how warm and cosy. In my opinion today's youth is missing so much. They ought to see this! What fun, what fun, to feel oneself back at one's parents' home for a short while. Suddenly you are fifty years back in time and feel the atmosphere of your parents, your five sisters, the living room, and especially the leaded glass windows. Everything surrounding you. Like a warm blanket.

We were allowed to take a candy, but I was afraid! I thought it was fun, and the candy tasted very nice (Gaia thought the sweets were 99 years old).

This is super fun!. Everything works, and you are allowed to touch and handle everything and it is very educational. This museum is a true marvel and it does look a lot like the past! My compliments! Laura, Albeda College, 1D

Today I have donated a vacuum cleaner from the fifties. What a wonderful museum and such a marvellous initiative. Congratulations. A world of childhood memories from opened up for my husband and myself. We have enjoyed ourselves with "the good old days". How beautifully you have copied the original. It is true what the tour-guide lady told us: you will leave here a happy person. Chapeau for everyone.

After almost five months of apprenticeship at the occupational-therapy department, today for the first time, accompanied by my parents and grandmother, I have had a look at the museum. It was a feast of recognition for them, and I myself now have a better perspective of how the clients and their families used to live in bygone days!

How wonderful to walk around and look at everything. I am dazzled. My sons, (14, 10, 9) are upstairs behind the computer and have been here before. But on the next visit, I will certainly bring them along again. We really, really, really like it very much, but we were really confronted with the fact that we recognized so many things! We'll certainly visit here again, every time I see something different.

The ladies from "De Hoeksteen" have very much enjoyed themselves. We missed seeing an "Aunt Betty". This is an old-fashioned coffee filter bag, with an iron thread. (we have since procured an Aunt Betty for the collection – H.B.)

It is just wonderful, what I have seen here! Have had some delightful conversations with visitors from Groningen (North of Holland). And rehashed the days of old. Was quite moved by all the familiar things from my youth. Just like that, on a Friday afternoon, going back in time! Recognizable, sentimental, for a moment the smell of the past! Very well done! Envious of the chair in the corner next to the radio.

Four giggling ladies thought that there was a lifesize doll sitting on the bench in the hall, but were shocked to find it was a "living doll". Hilarious!

The Oudheidkamer (Archaeology Chamber) from Pernis was present with management and personnel. We have thoroughly enjoyed ourselves and picked up some ideas to try out for ourselves.

Very nostalgic. Back to the forties again, with the grocery's opposite from our house in the North of Rotterdam, near the terminal of tramline 11. We have a lot of appreciation for the work you have done in this building. For so many people it is wonderful to see, feel and smell this again. Emotional, nostalgic, in admiration and awe, moving, being back in time. A memory of sleep-overs at my grandparents' house.

We have relived an old-fashioned and familiar Saturday evening with the radio on and shell-peanuts on the table. And there was the grocery's with such variety of hand soaps. It is fantastic. The laundry room, too, brought back happy memories. Wonderful, all those old things! The wooden blocks, the spoons and especially the old little fur bonnet.

We visited here with sisters and brothers between 57 and 78 years of age. Enjoyed everything and shared our experiences. Particularly because we have handled and touched everything. Which is not allowed anywhere else. Our day has been perfect! I myself will certainly return for a visit with one sister, who has been living abroad for many years now, and who will be able to revisit her old homeland here.

Beautiful, pure nostalgia! A wonderful destination for old-fashioned objects from our youth. When I am home I shall certainly search for things for here. They will find a good home here. My heart went out to the grocery store, because it is my trade, and because I have grown up on the premises, and I still work there.

My mother has dementia, but she was pointing out at so many things here. She cannot speak, but at one stage she was crying – I hope it was from recognition.

Care Home Innersdijk in Groningen: "We are so utterly jealous", how we would love to have a wonderful basement like yours! A lot of recognition, and fun to see it back again. I myself have a lot of my grandmother's old things. Now I know where they are glad to have them, so, off to the museum with them! Seen so many familiar things, and lots of "ooh yeah, I used to have one of those". And so beautifully designed!

For the Koops family it was their annual sibling-day. We have enjoyed ourselves tremendously, and had many beautiful memories of times past. A pity that we have all grown so much older, and are not as agile as we used to be, but plenty of chairs to take a moment's rest. Our compliments for the pretty lay-out!

One lady had a particularly nice memory from seeing the wash-board! Whenever she was ill she used to be allowed to lie down in her father's liberty-chair in the living room, which was a reclining chair. The wash board supported by the arms of the chair made a nice little playing-table, on which she also was served some tasty titbits.

I (75) had a granny. My granny used to have a small table in the kitchen with a piece of oil cloth. On that little table there was a little bowl. She used to fill it with the skins of the hot milk. At the end of the day she added some sugar and had herself a nice little meal.

Commentary on the dog-cart:

When I was a girl of four, maybe five years old, I once sat looking out of the window of our ground-floor apartment in Rotterdam, and saw the baker's cart coming down the street. The wheels rattled loudly over the cobbles, and some housewives were already waiting for him at their front doors. He stopped close to our house and produced his keys from his baker's apron and opened the lid of the cart. The lock was for protection from burglars. At that moment, about 16 hefty men (all skin and bones, mind you!) came running toward the baker, hit him over the head and as he went down bleeding, made off with the contents of the cart. I sat in my little chair, rigid, and screamed for my mother. She brought the man inside, cleaned the wound on his cheek, and his boss was warned. Later, every time I saw the baker, I could not help but look at the deep scar on his cheek and thought, you poor man! Forty years later I got to know someone via the internet, and she, miraculously, turned out to be the baker's daughter. I had,

in fact, recounted this story to one of the local Rotterdam papers. And she told me that her father had actually made a deal with these men to have himself robbed and clobbered over the head, because he felt so sorry for the poor citizens, and because his boss used to feed the left-over loaves of bread to the pigs in the afternoon. Right there and then I reassessed this wartime memory, and feel better for it.

Commentary on the game of donkey's tail:

I have some bad memories of our mantelpiece, dating from the time a was a five-year-old girl. It was my fifth birthday and my birthday party. All the presents were stacked on the mantelpiece, and they included a jar with guppies. And after the lemonade we went for some fun and games, like sack-racing and donkey's tail. When the party was over and I went to have a look at my presents, the guppies had been boiled in their jar, just because my birthday was in the winter and the fire had been on!

Commentary on the children's chasuble:
Roman Catholic mischief. With a twinkle in her eyes one lady recounts how she once put a little Reckitts Blue from her mother's kitchen in the holy water, and what a funny effect it had had; everybody came out of the church with a little blue spot on their forehead.

Commentary on the laundry room:
There used to be a lot of children who had to fetch a bucket of hot water from the 'waterstoker', which cost 2 cents. It was quite heavy to carry such a load back up the stairs, but I have always been proud of the fact that my mother gave me a special little plank to float on the water. It would stop the "spilling-over". And that was something other children did not have.

Commentary on the Maggi tin (the Dutch equivalent for Oxo cubes):
They were calling out for Emmy. When she had finally been found they were shouting: "Have a look, here's your tin!" With much hilarity a small round Maggi tin was held up in the air. It was explained to me that the two elder sisters had been instructed to baby-sit their younger sister Emmy, who, when they let their guard down for a moment, got her hand jammed inside the tin. The sisters got a telling off for not paying attention, after which they all went to the doctor's, who had a hard time prising the hand out of the tin.

There are also positive reponses frome abroad. A selection:

A wonderful museum that causes many emotions! Thank you, it was very interesting. From the group from Sweden. What a wonderful experience it was, to see all those things from years gone by!

Reckit Blue. Is used for washing, but in Surinam it is sometimes put on a baby's bum to ward off all evil.

The Israeli group of directors of old age homes of Eshel thank you for an amazing and interesting visit. You succeed to provide a high quality of life to those who are needy and we appreciate it.

We are visitors from Northern Alberta, Canada. We emigrated from Holland in 1958 and our relatives invited us to visit this very interesting and unusual museum. We enjoyed our visit and highly recommend it to everyone. The information and showing by very capable personel was excellent and we enjoyed it very much.

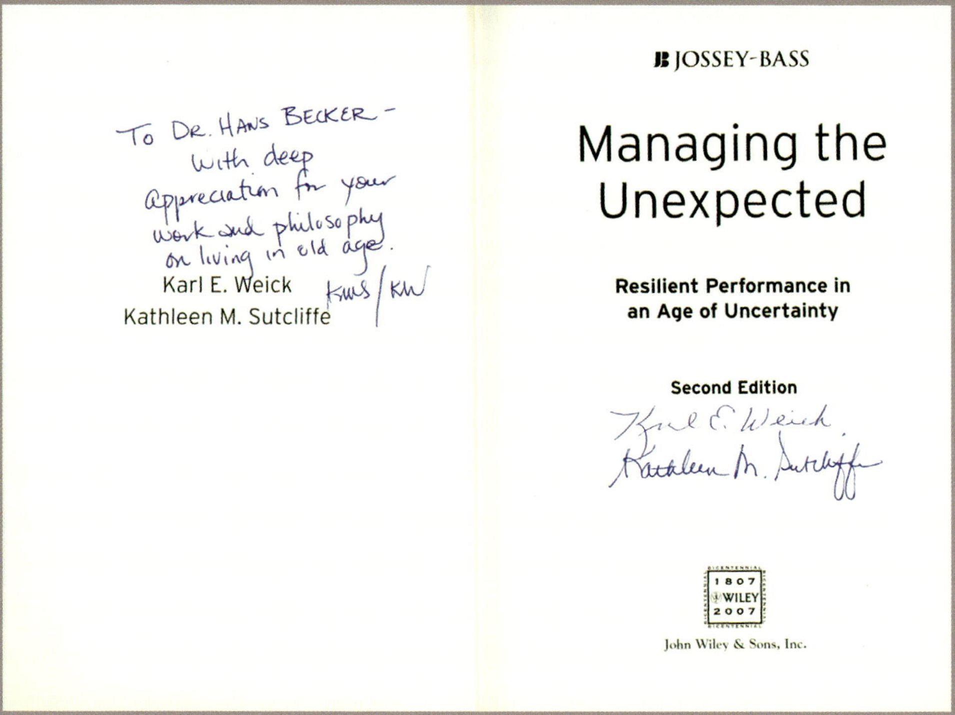

Reactions about the philosophy and museum reached us even from the Unites States, and not just from anybody, but from Professor Karl Weick, well-known for his theory of cultural steering, who sent us a signed copy of his latest edition

THE HON JUSTINE ELLIOT MP

Minister for Ageing

MEDIA RELEASE

26 June 2008

'Apartments for Life' innovative Dutch model lets 95 per cent of older people stay in their own homes

Minister for Ageing, Mrs Justine Elliot today met with Humanitas Foundation, an innovative Dutch housing model which allows 95 per cent of older people to live in their own homes until the end of their lives. This is known as "ageing in place."

The "Apartments for Life" model was developed by renowned academic Dr Hans Becker who is currently touring Australia.

Barbara Squires, General Manager - Ageing, Benevolent Society was also at the meeting.

The Humanitas Foundation, which began in 1995, now manages 1000 apartments which are built to be "age proof" so they can accommodate wheelchairs and nursing home type care, if required – in response to the changing needs of residents.

After a meeting with Dr Becker in Canberra, Mrs Elliot said the Australian aged care industry could examine this project – which enables individual control, social support, community connection and appropriate housing design.

"It enables the great majority of its residents to stay in their homes. This is what older Australians, and especially ageing baby boomers, tell us they want," Mrs Elliot said.

The Benevolent Society of Australia, which sponsored the study tour, will prepare a report on the outcomes.

Justine Elliot - Minister for Ageing, Barbara Squires – Benevolent Society, Dr Hans Becker - Humanitas Foundation

For more information, contact Mrs Elliot's office on (02) 6277 7280

The Australian Federal Government even put out a press release regarding the Humanitas system approach, of which the reminiscence museum is an important integral part

The hot-water bottle and foot stoves collection

A hot-water bottle and foot heater collector from The Hague donated his complete collection of over one hundred, sometimes very rare, specimens. The collection is on display in one of our Humanitas establishments

footstool bottle

car bottle

bottle with room for heating baby-bottle

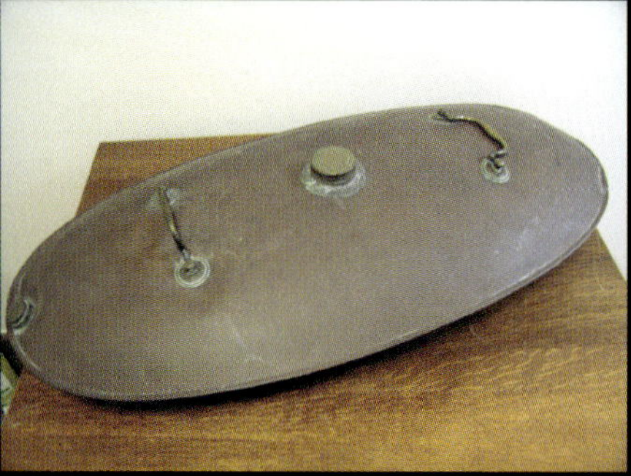
communal orphan's bottle

pastor's footstool bottle

coachman's bottle

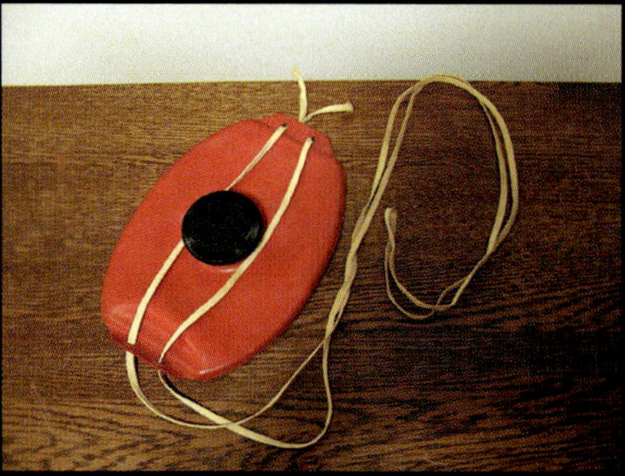
stomach bottle

little muff's bottles (to keep hands warm)

church foot warmers

carriage warmer

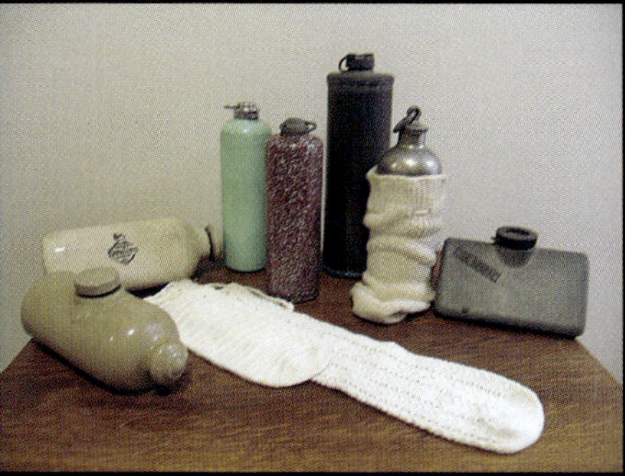

church warmer

hand warmers

heated bricks

oil heated bottles

The wheelchair collection

The Humanitas wheelchair collection from all over Europe. Over the last years the collection has expanded by purchase and donations, and is growing, still

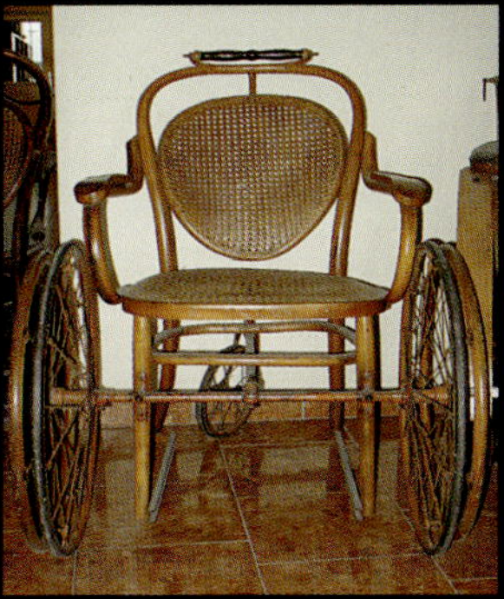
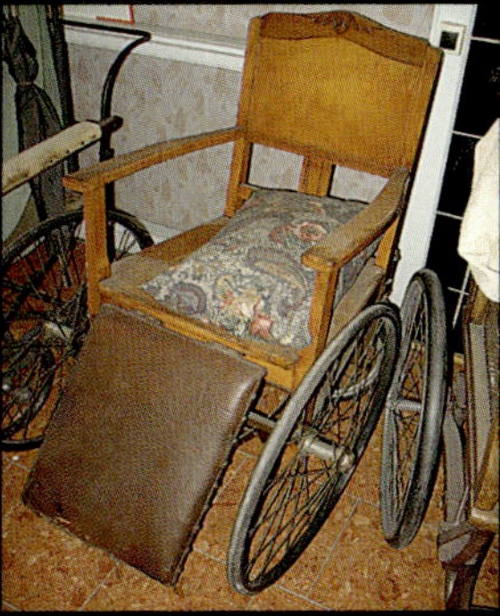

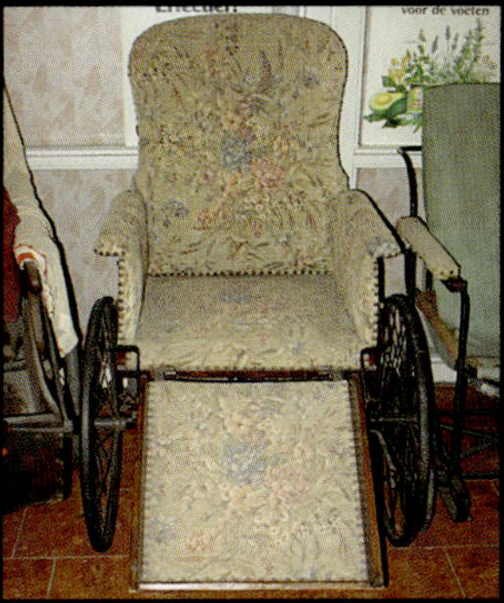

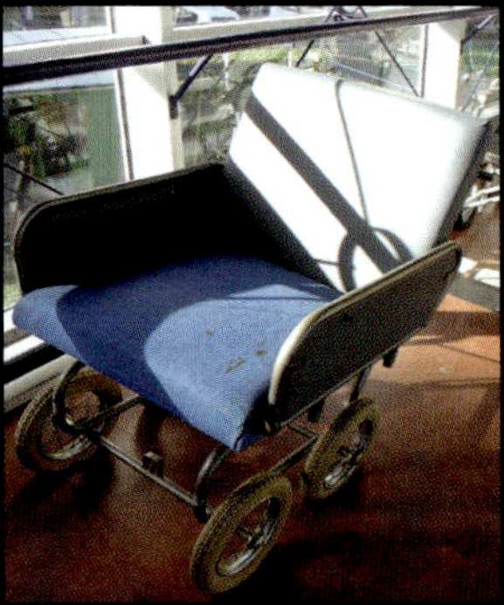

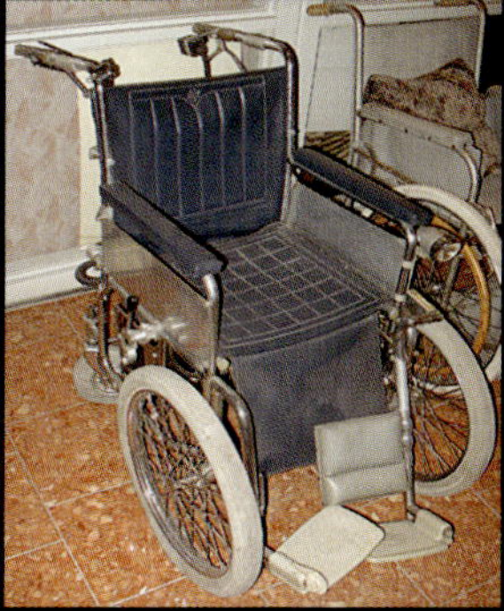

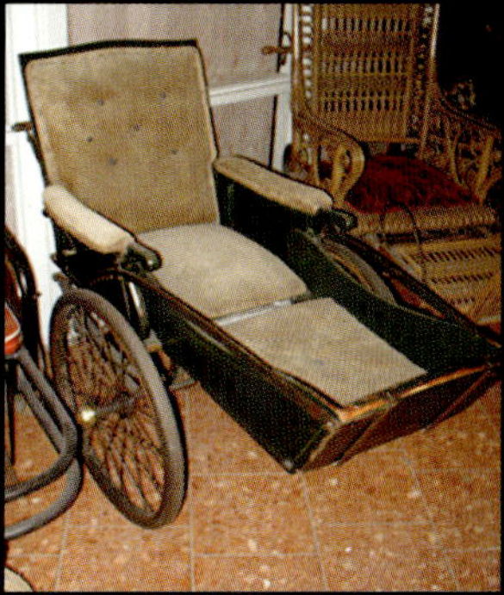

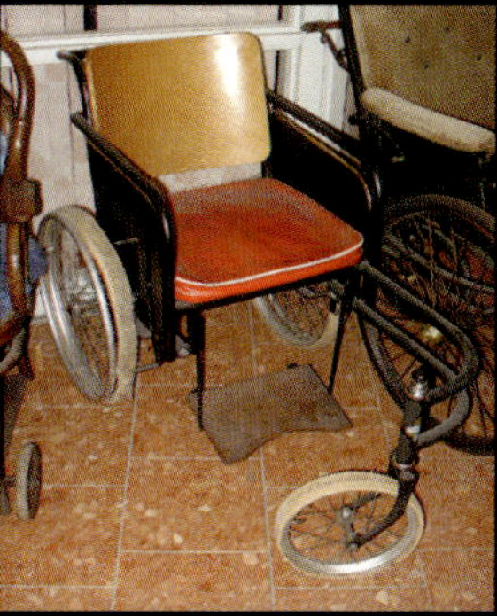

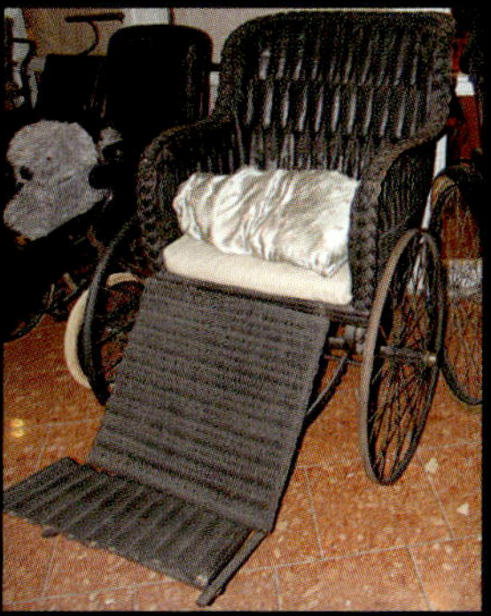

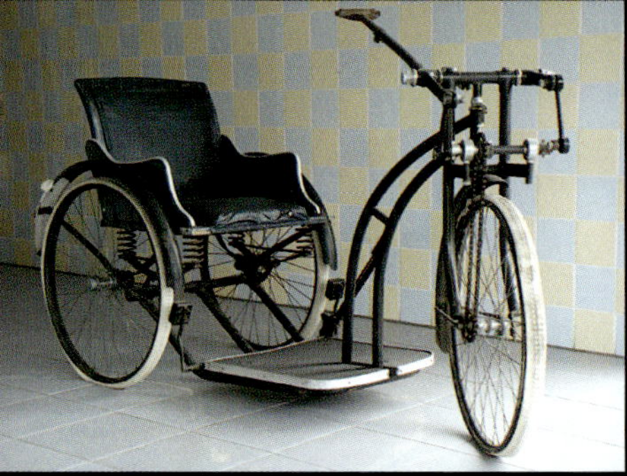

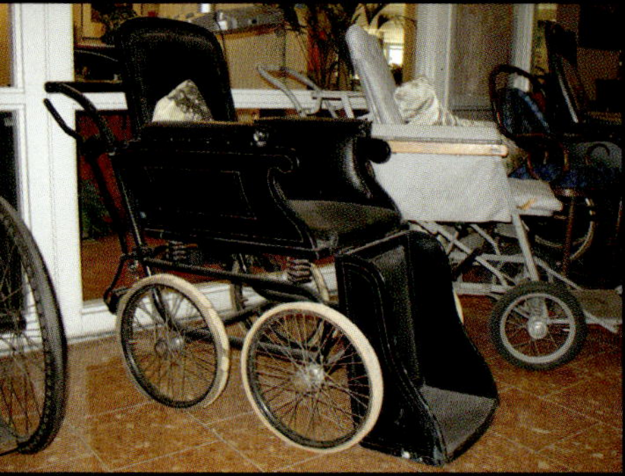
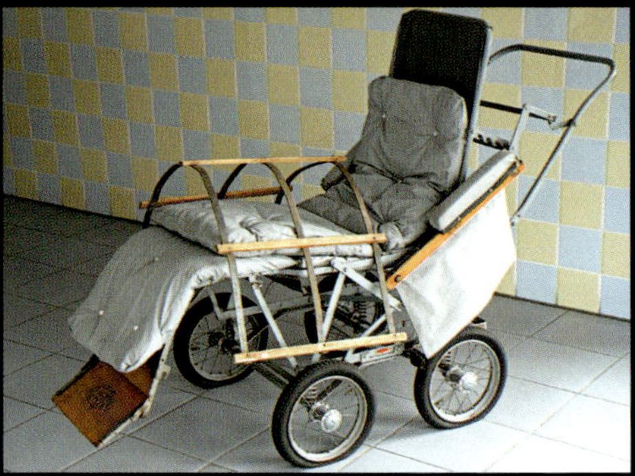

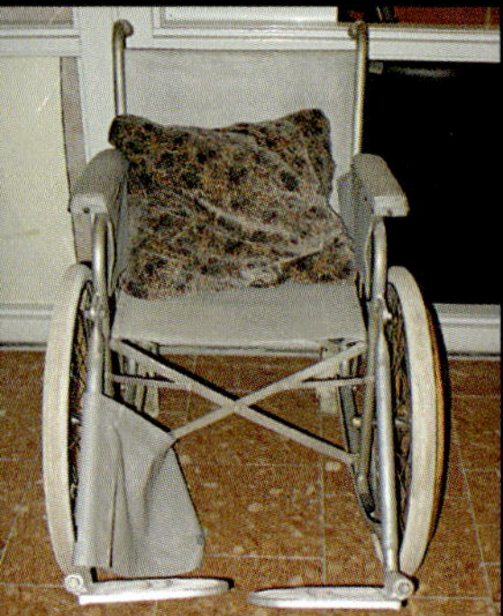

VONKVRIJ.VEILIG
VéGé
LANTAARN
VEILIGHEIDS
LUCIFERS
MOLEN
LUCIFERS
KROON LUCIFERS
NEDERLANDSCH FABRIKAAT
VEILIGHEIDSLUCIFERS
SÄKERHETS TÄNDSTICKOR
PARAFFINERADE
TRADE-MARK
SVALAN
THE SWALLOW
DIE SCHWALBE
DE ZWALUW
MANUFACTURED AT UDDEVALLA
TÄNDSTICKSFABRIK, SWEDEN.
ZWALUW SINDS 1895
ANNEKE HAALT HOUT VOOR HET FORNUIS. MOEDER STRIJKT
EEN "ZWALUW" AAN, WANT HET IS KOUD IN HUIS

OUBLE SIX
FABRIQUÉ
EN BELGIQUE
ALLUMETTES DE SURETÉ
THE VICTORIA
IMPREGNATED SAFETY MATCHES
MADE IN BELGIUM
Uitvinders
2e serie 26-50
SPA
ERHETS TÄNDSTICKOR
PARAFFINERADE
TRADE-MARK
THE SWALLOW
DE ZWALUW
FACTURED AT UDDEVALLA
OSTICKSFABRIK, SWEDEN.
Sponsor
lucifers
STER-LUCIFERS
lucifers
27
lstra

Some examples of museum ground plans

**Reminiscence museums can have various ground plans. However, it is important to consider these beforehand: cellar museum, entrance museum, restaurant museum, one room museum and corridor museum.
Some examples:**

Entrance museum Hannie Dekhuijzen

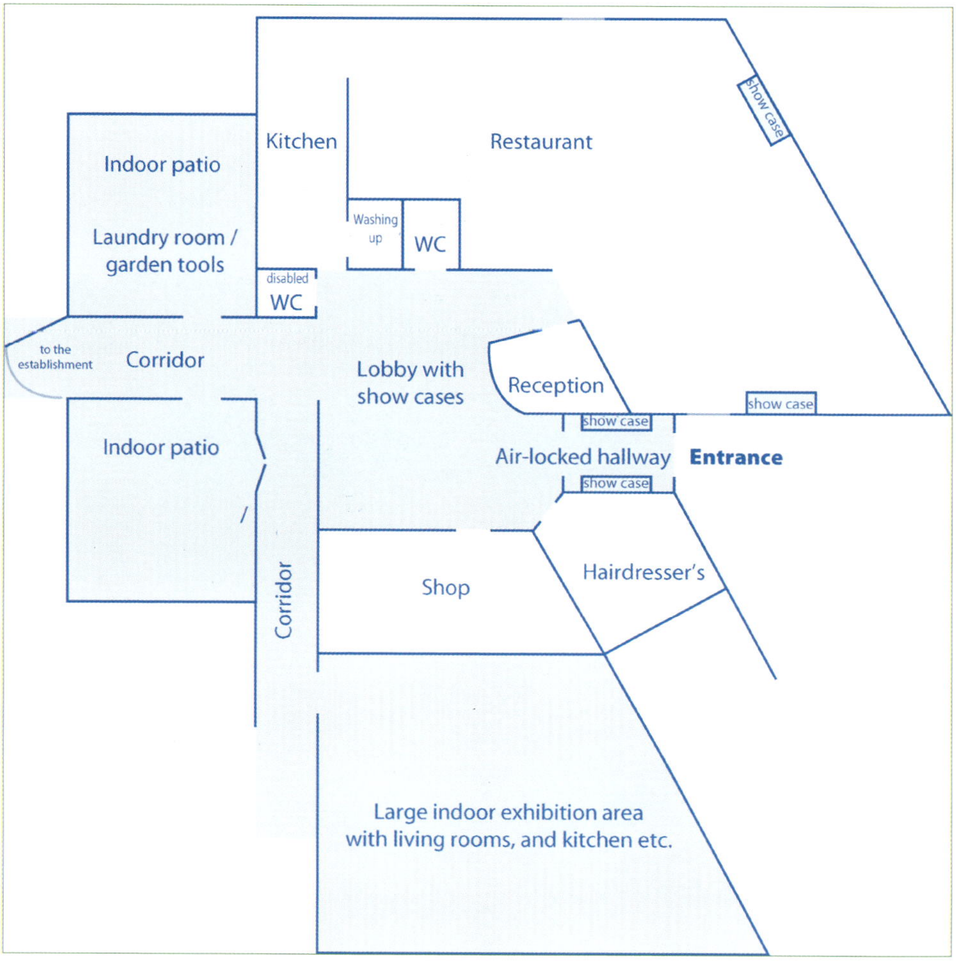

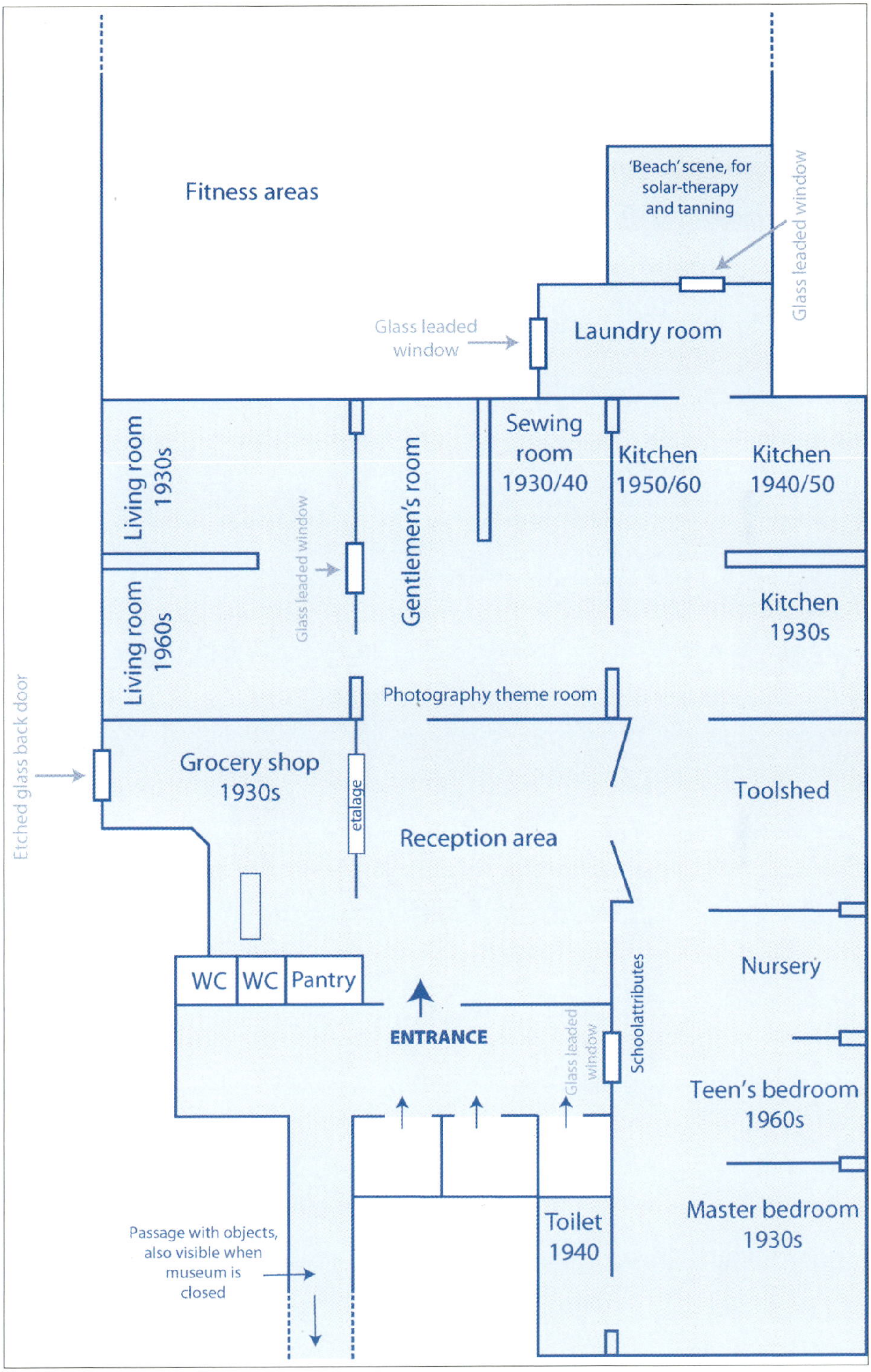
Fitness areas
'Beach' scene, for solar-therapy and tanning
Glass leaded window
Glass leaded window
Laundry room
Living room 1930s
Sewing room 1930/40
Kitchen 1950/60
Kitchen 1940/50
Glass leaded window
Gentlemen's room
Kitchen 1930s
Living room 1960s
Photography theme room
Etched glass back door
Grocery shop 1930s
etalage
Toolshed
Reception area
Nursery
WC
WC
Pantry
ENTRANCE
Glass leaded window
Schoolattributes
Teen's bedroom 1960s
Master bedroom 1930s
Toilet 1940
Passage with objects, also visible when museum is closed

Corridor museum Gerard Goosenflat with outer corridor, separated by display cases

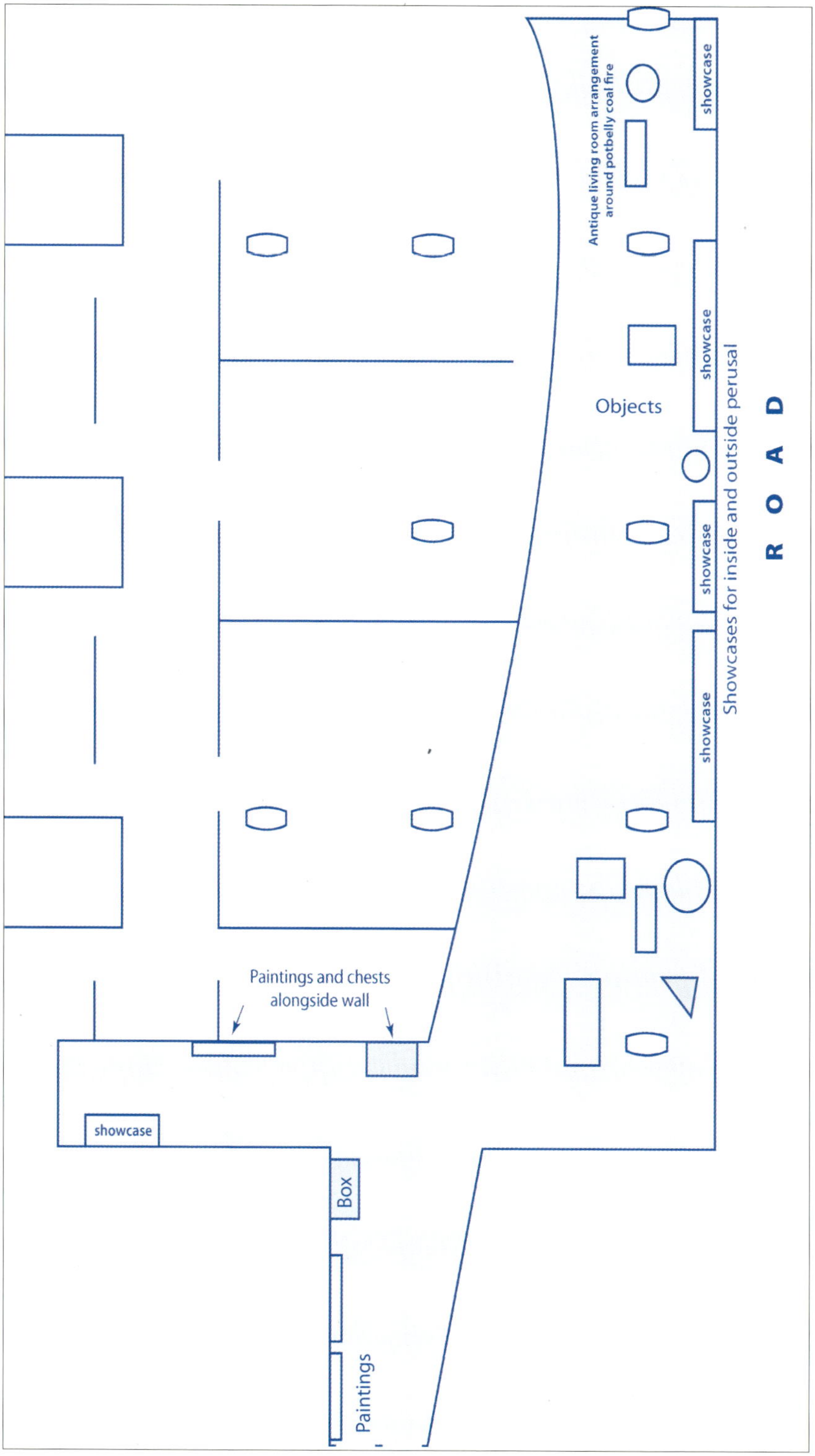

Cellar museum Jan Meertensflat

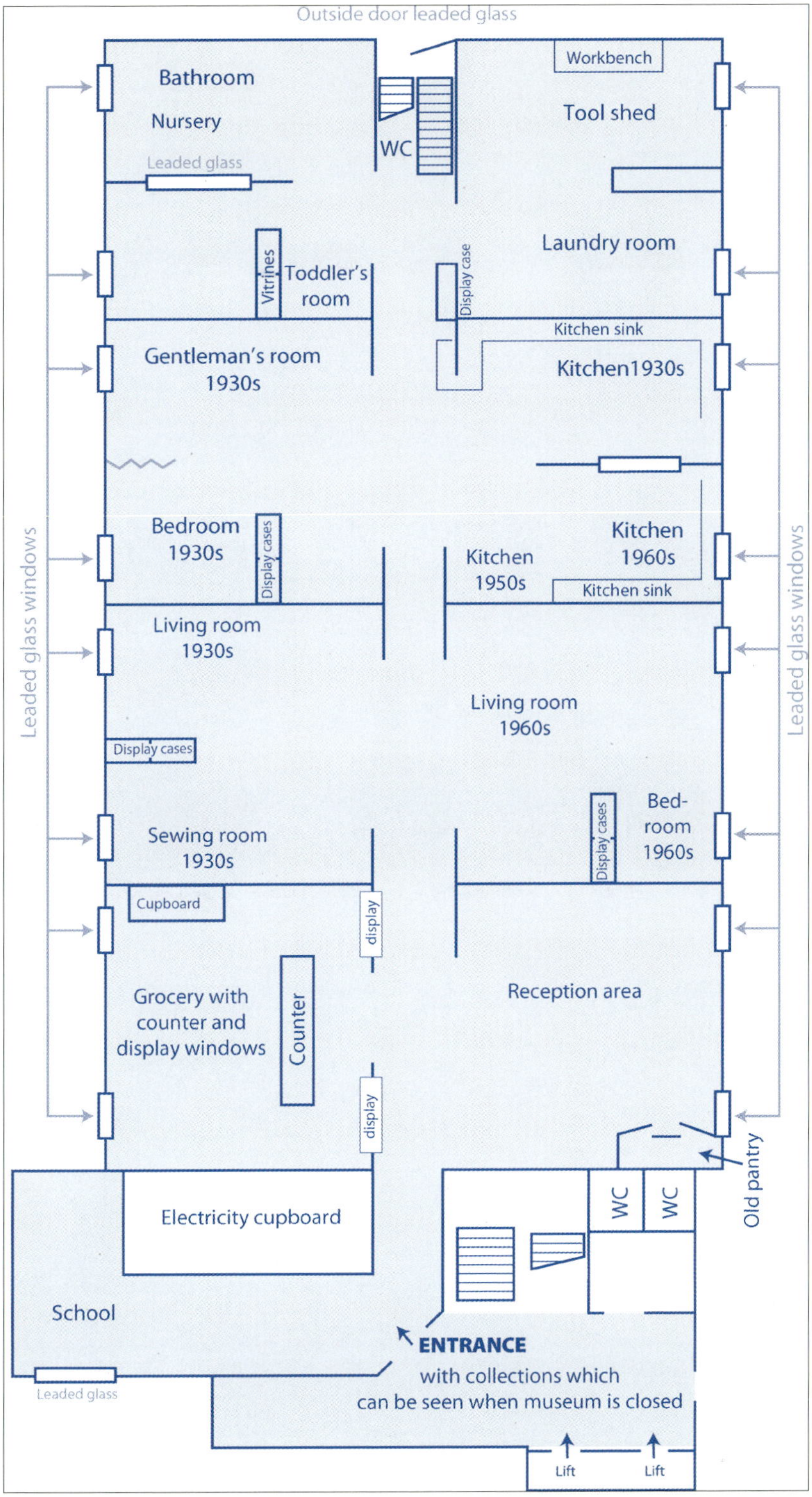

What is this?!

Reminiscence Museum Humanitas -Akropoli

It is better to make the visitors curious and let them try to find out the meaning of the objects by themselves. The decoupling is much stronger than presented on a program.

What is this?! THE ANSWERS

01 GAS LIGHTER
02 GLOVES EXTENDER
03 INSECT REPELLENT
04 POCKET KNIFE WITH BODKIN (FORMERLY USED BY SAILORS TO SPLIT ROPE)
05 CHERRY-PIP REMOVER
06 AIR RAID (**IDENTIFICATION??) BAND (WORN IN WARTIME DURING AIR-RAIDS)
07 LIME KETTLE (USED TO MAKE GLUE FROM BONES)
08 SIRENS
09 SPANNER
10 MORSE ENCODER (FOR SIGNALLING MESSAGES)
11 APPLIANCE TO MAKE D.I.Y. CIGARETS WITH CRUDE TOBACCO, AND EMPTY CARTRIDGES
12 SHAVING BLADE SHARPENER
13 GARBAGE MAN'S RATTLE
14 ROLLER SWEEP FOR USE ON THE TABLE
15 PAINT SPRAYER (TO BE MOUNTED ON THE BLOW-END OF A VACUUM CLEANER)
16 SHEARS (ALSO USED FOR THATCHING ROOFS)
17 PHOTO DEVELOPER TANK
18 MAGIC LANTERN (PREDECESSOR OF THE SLIDES PROJECTOR)
19 EGG POACHER
20 CARBIDE LANTERN
21 SMALL MANUAL WOOD SHAVER
22 UNDULATING IRON, OR TONGS (TO MAKE WAVING CURLS IN HAIR)
23 SHAVING KNIFE GRINDER
24 APPLIANCE FOR MAKING WOODEN BARRELS, OR TUBS
25 WHETTING STONE (FOR GRINDING CHISELS, KNIVES ETC)
26 "DIEFJE"(" LITTLE THIEF") – LAMP FITTING WITH EXTRA THREE-WAY PLUG
27 PLUMMET (TO MARK VERTICAL LINES ON WALLS)
28 APPLIANCE TO PREVENT BOILING MILK FROM SPILLING OVER
29 LOUD SPEAKER FOR DISTRIBUTION RADIO (USED DURING AND JUST AFTER THE WAR)
30 DISTRIBUTION RADIO (ACCOMPANIES 29)
31 HOSING DEVICE TO CLEAN WINDOWS (PLACE IN PAIL AND PUMP UP WATER)
32 CURLING TONGS (SEE ALSO 22)
33 BOOT-JACK (AID TO TAKE OFF ONE'S BOOTS)
34 DARNING EGG (FOR DARNING SOCKS)
35 HEMLINE MARKER (SPRAYS CHALK-LINE TO MARK LENGTH OF SKIRT OR CLOTHING)

THE REMINISCENCE MUSEUM WAS WIDELY PUBLISHISED IN THE MEDIA.
NEWSPAPERS, MAGAZINES, TELEVISION AND MANY INTERNET SITES PAID ATTENTION TO THIS NEW INNOVATIVE PHENOMENON.
THE PRIME TIME EIGHT O'CLOCK NEWS SPENT MANY MINUTES ON IT.

HET PAROOL
Trouw
De Telegraaf
Komt het Paleis gereed vóór het bezoek van Koning Leopold?
Koningin komt op 10 Juni kijken
„EEN WONDER"
ALS RESTAURATIE OP
Drie Nederlandse opvarenden gewond
vliegtuig
bij
1893

LEVENSKUNST op leeftijd

GELUK BEVORDERENDE ZORG IN EEN VERGRIJZENDE WERELD

Prof.dr. Hans Marcel Becker

Eburon

The Humanitas Philosophy

Selection of the Humanitas one-liners

- A nice dinner is more effective and cheaper than a boring meeting
- Care is priced at a minimum of fifty euro cents per minute, well-being is cheaper and often more effective.
- Do not take care of people, just take care that they take care of themselves. So: "care, with the hands at your back"
- A barkeeper may be as important as a physician
- Money is never a problem when a plan is good, therefore never start out with money.
- "Well, that's Humanitas for you!"
- Use it or lose it
- No dietician's dictatorship
- Sick a little, work a little
- We have a yes-culture here
- No misery-islands
- The mangy mongrel may be just as important as the nurse

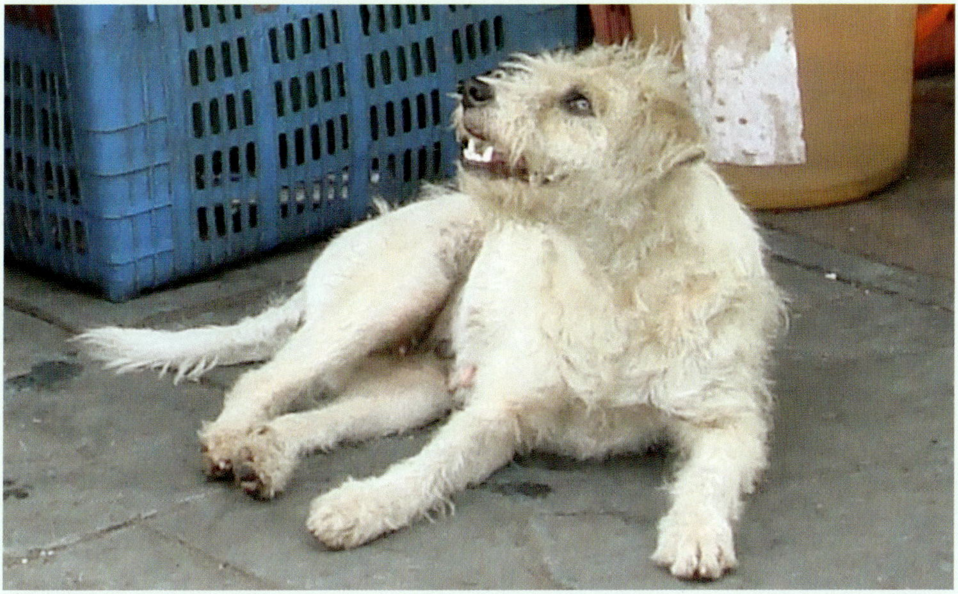

A summary of the Humanitas Philosophy

The starting point, as well as the ultimate goal of the Humanitas care philosophy is the enhancement of human happiness for clients with a physical, or somatic handicap. Cure and care are, therefore, no longer the core business. Living arrangements and a general feeling of well-being are elements of equal importance, or probably more so. In any case, cure and care should no longer be the defining factors for the atmosphere and general outlook. Human happiness is defined by two aspects, an individual aspect (a person, though handicapped, wishes to have control over his own life) and a communal aspect (a person needs to have a sense of belonging, is in fact a herd animal). This is what the care organization needs to focus on. And if cure and care is contributing to achieve this, it would be a bonus, but in that case extra attention should be given to the possible negative side effects of a medical/hygienic approach. Should the "pain" of cure and care prove greater than the "gain", it is probably better to abandon the cure and care, and concentrate on the well-being which causes the handicaps to be forgotten and the client to "learn to live" with a chronic handicap. In this way, well-being as an alternative for cure and care can be implemented reasonably often.
W==ith regards to the living arrangements, Humanitas, in view of the indi-

The Humanitas use it or lose it-focus

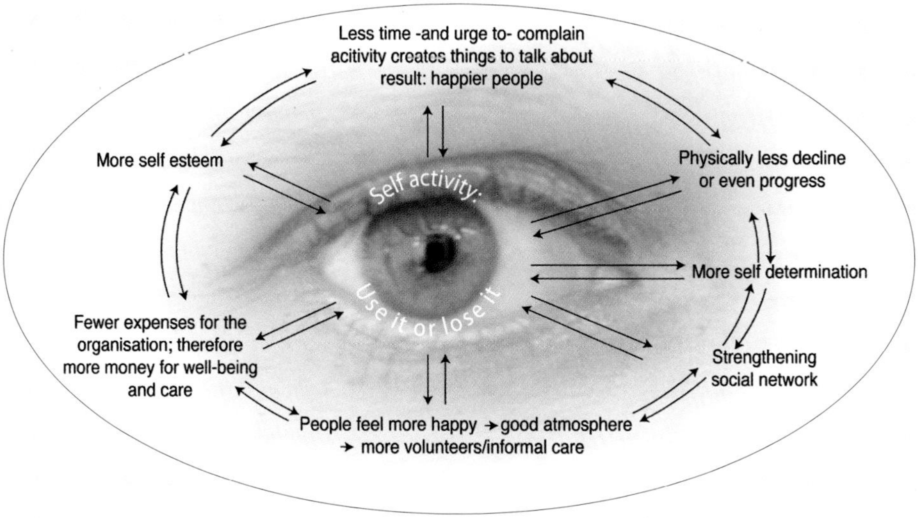

vidual wish for independency, has developed the "age-proof" apartments. These apartments (minimum 72 square metres, three rooms – the social norm for building requirements in the Netherlands), may be purchased, or hired out of one's own income. Which allows the client to be a true resi-

No dietician's dictatorship, but self direction

Not "they", the patients who are unable to fend for themselves, and "we" the white coated professionals who think they know better than "them"

The yes-culture with service for every taste

dent, instead of just "staying" in a room belonging to an institution. Living arrangements and care should be strictly separate. In principle, the client should be able to choose a care provider, other than Humanitas. The landlord, in case of renting, might be Humanitas Housing, but could well be another housing corporation. Technically, the apartments should be designed in such a way that – even with a wheelchair – the sink (variable height sinks), the fuseboard, and the letterbox, are within reach, and barriers such as thresholds, narrow doorways, awkwardly opening French doors, etc, etc, are avoided.

Living arrangements, as a total living concept, do not only contribute to the individual aspect of happiness, but also to the communal aspect (the sense of "belonging"). To be a person amongst people, you need to meet people, mingle, share something: dine in the restaurant, eat apple pie, or have a drink at the bar, go to the hairdresser, the pedicure or the beauty parlour, visit the animal garden with the grandchildren, the sculpture garden, play bridge together, participate in volunteer work, go to the fitness for a daily work-out, or visit the reminiscence museum. You need sufficient space for this, a space which is created by the "sheltered" at the so-called "skirting board", on the lower level of the building. Naturally, the old cure and care elements, such as personal care, nursing, occupational therapy, a psychologist, social worker, dietician, indoor physician, speech therapist, and activity training attendance, are important. These services are also to be found in the village square. But on no account should these elements dominate the scene: so, no walking around in a white coat, no jungle of sign posts, no abundance of rules and regulations, no typical institute furniture, no fluorescent lighting. For there is little to cure, and regulate about chronic deceases like Alzheimer's, Parkinson's, arthritis, multiple sclerosis, or total old-age asthenisation. More often than not, the attention needs to be taken away from the handicaps and it is up to the organization to focus the attention on whatever pleasantness life still has to offer, on what is in fact still possible. The ongoing pre-occupation with medical and hygienic issues, setting rules, and discussions at all levels (nurse, dietician, indoor physician, speech therapist, occupational therapist, social worker, psychologist etc.) on these subjects will cause a negative atmosphere into the bargain! Constant accentuation of medical issues will cause what is left of a positive image of life to disappear, and institutions for the elderly will degenerate into what Becker Sr. (96) calls: "misery islands".

"I dont't know if my children should dine at Humanitas, they are from such humble descent.."

Regarding the management structure, Humanitas has chosen for a model which does not endorse a top-down hierarchy, but is characterized by a collective cultural operation (Prof. Karl Weick, USA), where all involved – managers, employees, clients, volunteer workers, relatives, suppliers – need to be aware of the core-values, and act accordingly. In this way some kind of empowerment is being created in the lower layers of the organization, and it will allow for bottom-up creativity and innovation. The core-values, therefore, are of the utmost importance for a properly functioning organization.

They are:

'Use it ore lose it"

Being in control of your own life Anyone, whose brains are still functioning, can decide for himself what is important to him, even if it implies matters, which are not commonly condoned. (being drunk at the bar every day, having a shower once every three weeks, wanting to keep five cats when that is really no longer an option).

•

Active participation. Of the utmost importance and clearly disregarded in care-industry. Once the basic functions (walking, making a cup of tea, keeping the finances in order, mending clothes, cooking) cease, these abilities will, before long, vanish in thin air. If one should stop walking for two months, regaining the ability will become almost impossible. So one needs, use it or lose it, to stay active. Becker senior set the limit: "to the pain-threshold". This is why Humanitas uses the slogans: "Too much care is worse than too little care", and

The Humanitas Temple of the Art of Living

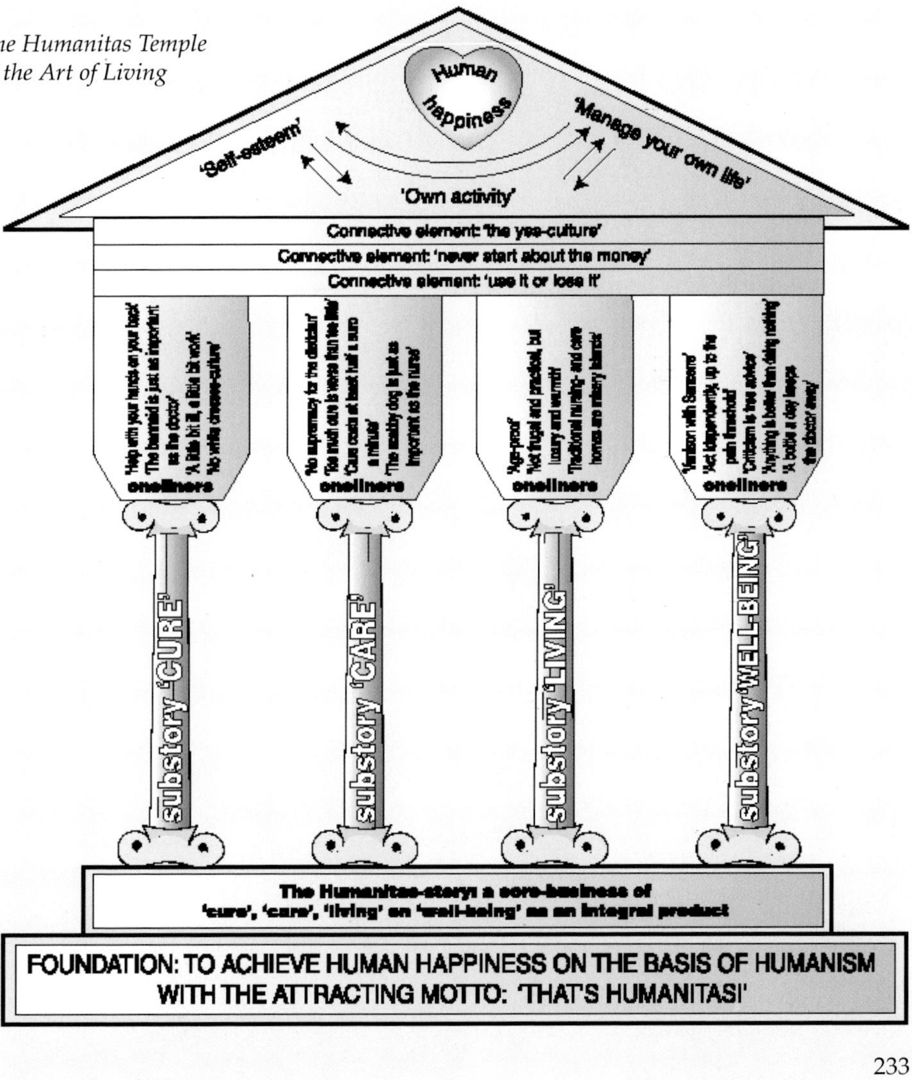

"Do not take care of people, but take care that they take care of themselves!" Naturally, the latter has its limits, and the carer would do well to be watchful. One cannot possibly ask a patient with paralysis to wash his own toes.

- *Extended family approach*. This implies that people should regard themselves as one big family, and not as "them", the handicapped, dying patients who have little awareness and few abilities, and "us", the altruistic, white-coated professionals, who after a few years of study think they know everything much better than "them". Those "them" who, as a matter of fact, have been experiential experts for over forty years and, together with their partner or extended family, know almost all there is to know about their handicaps.

- The fourth core-value, ***the yes-culture,*** is the driving force and indicator. It creates the positive atmosphere and activating ambiance. The yes-culture means that all concerned (management, employee, relative, client, volunteer worker) will have a positive attitude towards any request concerning the wish to be in control, active participation or funny ideas, questions or demands. If the request can not be met forthright, a dialogue will be started with the requesting client. Not to argue in order to win, but to enquire, in an open manner,

The Humanitas Extended Family

which motivations prompted the request, whether there are any alternatives, and how the care organization might come to an agreement with the client in a service-rendering, positive way.
The abovementioned elements, such as real-life restaurants, also attracting public from outside and where everyone can place an order using their own money, the reminiscence museums providing topics of conversation for everyone, as well as the hairdresser, beauty parlour, the animal farm etc., are meant to enhance the positive and activating atmosphere even more. What matters is the totality of atmosphere and ambiance. The sum total of cure and care, well-being and living arrangements is an integral product, one cannot exist without the other.

On entering an establishment of the Humanitas care organization, one should as it were be taken by surprise by the exhilarating, warm, happy, activating company culture. Actually, the totality of colours, smells, sounds, artefacts, and people "going about their business", should in no way remind us of "care". Usually the care organizations are associated with hygiene, medication, rules, and mortality. These elements are, of course, ever present, but should be offered rather covertly. The mainstream should consist of the happy things in life.

One of the last on the list of elements to be mentioned, is the blending. In principle, handicaps and misery should not be clustered. Misery islands are easily created, even if it is not deliberate. Therefore, Humanitas makes an effort to blend: sick and healthy (at least one third of the residents must not have a care indication), young and old, rich and poor, native and ethnic minorities, homosexual and heterosexual. This kind of blending is extended to drawing the neighbourhood residents in from outside. The "catch" is realized by an excellent and reasonably priced restaurant, a good physiotherapist, a neighbourhood supermarket, a beauty parlour, a hairdresser, a cash point, an internet café, enough space for a large bridge club, a nursery for the whole neighbourhood, etc.

By creating an altogether happy picture, Humanitas is able to attract employment more easily, with less personnel falling off, and it is simpler to obtain a lower sick-leave rating, the relatives visit more often. Likewise, Humanitas has a magnetic appeal to volunteer workers, clients are less prone to depression, and are active participants, assisted by their partner. Clients are also helping each other, instead of calling upon the help of the rather scarce professional "hands at the bedside". All available competence is employed, including all experiential expertise and activating human characteristics. In this way all (financial) capacity is being used and expensive care demands, which are often just a cry for attention in the traditional misery islands, are prevented.

A vision on volunteer workers

It is important to have a vision on volunteer work, even for the museum volunteer worker. The following vision is a revised and summarized survey of Becker's book "The Art of Living in Later Life", which is interpreted here from the point of view of the museum volunteer workers

Volunteer workers and the different kinds of voluntary care.
Humanitas, which includes its nation-wide Society as well as its Foundation, has a wealth of volunteer workers at its disposal. The Humanitas Rotterdam Foundation has about eleven hundred volunteer workers employed in various fields. Many of them are at work in the care, but also in administration, at the art exhibitions, at the borrow-a-pet service, in the restaurants, in the garden upkeep, making house calls, in the internet corners, looking after the animals and plants and, last but not least: at the reminiscence museums.

Palette of Humanitas volunteer work

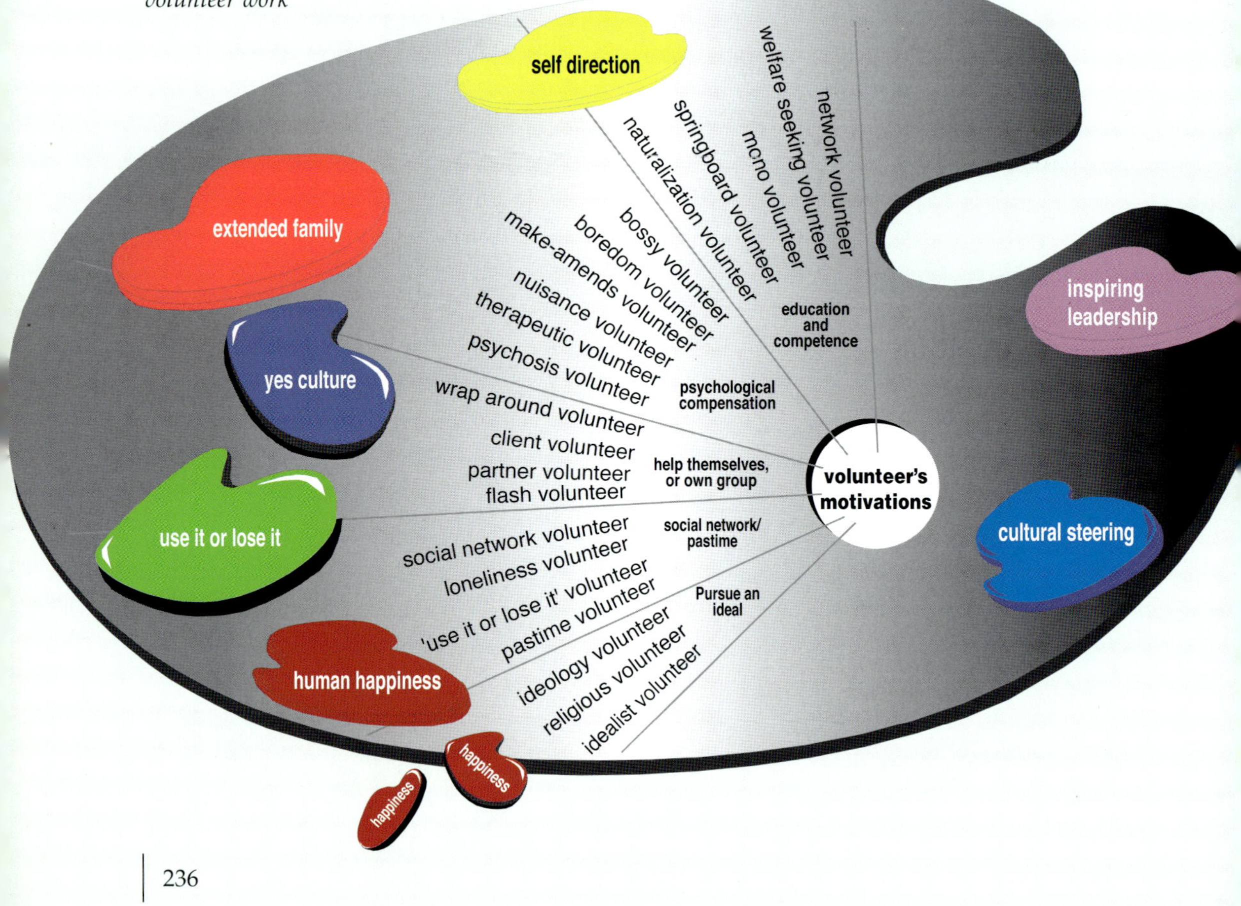

The internet volunteer

A survey done by the "Sociaal en Cultureel Planbureau" (the Social and Cultural Planning Office) shows that despite the apparent extensive and divers standards of participation in club life and volunteer work in the Netherlands, there is little concrete information available about the actual behavioural patterns of active citizens within these organizations, their networks, careers and backgrounds. The question arises what motivations these people have to take care of one another, without the coercion of law, contractual obligations, or economical necessity.

The children's farm volunteer

Humanitas believes that it is indeed vital to know the motivations of each and every individual volunteer worker. In order to find the right setting, to be inviting and stimulating for each individual, the organization needs to have their relevant personal background information at its disposal. (*) Managing Director Van Baar, of the "Hofstichting" in The Hague, commented in relation to this that there is no shortage in volunteer workers, but rather a shortage in organizations to inspire them.

Underlying motivations of volunteer work.
L. Willems has stated that the voluntary care for one another is one of the fundamental characteristics of the primary social behaviour patterns people live by: the family, the extended family and the circle of friends and acquaintances. The author of this book endeavours, with his extended family approach, to anticipate and address these primary social behavioural patterns and heartily agrees that service-rendering and support are often rooted in compassion and a sense of solidarity.
However, there are many other roots leading to volunteer work, than the often individually defined ones. Willems defines volunteer work in general as work done without obligation and without payment, in some organized fashion, on behalf of others, or the society. There is an ongoing discussion whether "without obligation and without payment" are always a sign of true altruism.

The altruism/egotism debate will, according to Willems, result in most authors interpreting various behavioural patterns, which might seem altruistic on the surface, as in fact defined by egoism. But there are other authors, such as Sen and Wakefield, who are willing to allow room for dedication to a greater good through conviction and without occupying oneself with personal gain. In what might be called pseudo-altruistic statements from volunteer workers, a number of possibilities are distinguishable: volunteer work to rid oneself from negative feelings when realizing that others are in clear misery, to prevent feelings of shame and guilt, or to gain social standing and boost one's self-esteem.

But in practice the effectiveness will be the same, whether volunteer work is done from motivations of egotism or altruism. It is, however, prudent for the organizations working with volunteer workers to make a thorough assessment of the underlying motivations, in order to address them. A number of authors have charted the motivations for volunteer work. To this palette, the author of this book will venture to add his own contribution.

The bar, and restaurant volunteer

The administration volunteer

Clary and Snyder distinguish four different inner motivating functions for volunteer work. Humanitas has seen them all put into practice, and they are:

- Value-expressing function: when doing volunteer work, the wish to express one's social and humanitarian involvement is being met.
- Social-adaptation function: when doing volunteer work, the wish to extend one's social network or social appreciation is being met.
- Knowledge function: when doing volunteer work, the wish to acquire knowledge is being met.
- Ego-defensive function: when doing volunteer work, the need to compensate for what is otherwise lacking in life is being met.

Sherrot has a somewhat different perspective on the matter and accentuates the search for diversion, social contacts and relaxation. Reasons founded on morals or norms are distinguished as: "natural helpers", people for whom, by their standards of reciprocity, lending a helping hand to their neighbours and neighbourhood is a matter of course;

The piano volunteer

"noblesse oblige", the better-off need to help the less well-off in society; "religiously inspired" helpers; and "guilt-dischargers" who, for instance, are doing voluntary care work because in the past they neglected their own mother in her old age.

When Drucker described the ideal employee as being: 'most dedicated people are ultimately volunteers' it aligns with the extended family-vision of Humanitas. Even regular employees need to be gifted with some kind of volunteering spirit.

Not only theoretically but in practice, too, volunteer work tends to merge smoothly with non-voluntary work.

The importance of volunteer work for Humanitas.

Volunteer workers being very important to the Humanitas organization, need not come as a surprise: eleven hundred motivated and enthusiastic people working for next to nothing, some even full-time, not only provide a financial gain for the organization, but are an asset for the total corporate culture. All in all very compelling reasons to get along well with one's volunteer workers.

The statement in Willems' interesting study "Burgerzin en vrijwillige zorg" ("Civil duty and voluntary care") where one may conclude that organized voluntary care, however valuable, may often fall short for various reasons, can be endorsed by Humanitas from practical experience. All the more reason to apply the services of volunteer workers in the right place, with the right support, this way neutralizing any negative effects. This has also been of great importance to the volunteer workers at the reminiscence museum. To find the right niche, one needs to find out what the volunteer worker is really looking for. Volunteer workers, like regular personnel, are prone to good and bad habits, their pros an cons. Like everyone else, they have their own agenda. As with regular personnel, one needs to find the right man for the right spot. Fortunately, not all volunteer workers are looking for the same things.

The theatre volunteer

The Becker way of volunteer worker classification.

The author has tried to chart and classify the different kinds of volunteers working for Humanitas. Bear in mind that a volunteer worker may exhibit a variety of aspects and, therefore, needs to be evaluated from different angles for appropriate classification. Humanitas classification elements are:

a. Ideal seeking
b. Social network / pastime seeking
c. Psychological compensation seeking
d. Learning and competence seeking
e. Helping family, or own (social or ethnic) group

Ad a. The first category is the volunteer worker pursuing an ideal. One of the popular kinds of volunteer workers is the *idealist-volunteer*, who devotes himself out of idealism, in total disregard of time, money and means, in order to realize his ideals. The volunteer / curator at Humanitas, for instance, could be an example for this category. The kind of volunteer who approaches the *ideology-volunteer*. The kind which could be highly suitable for the institution, and indeed, often is. Problems may arise when the individually perceived ideal appears to deviate from the collective ideal, as recorded in the *corporate*

The sport volunteer

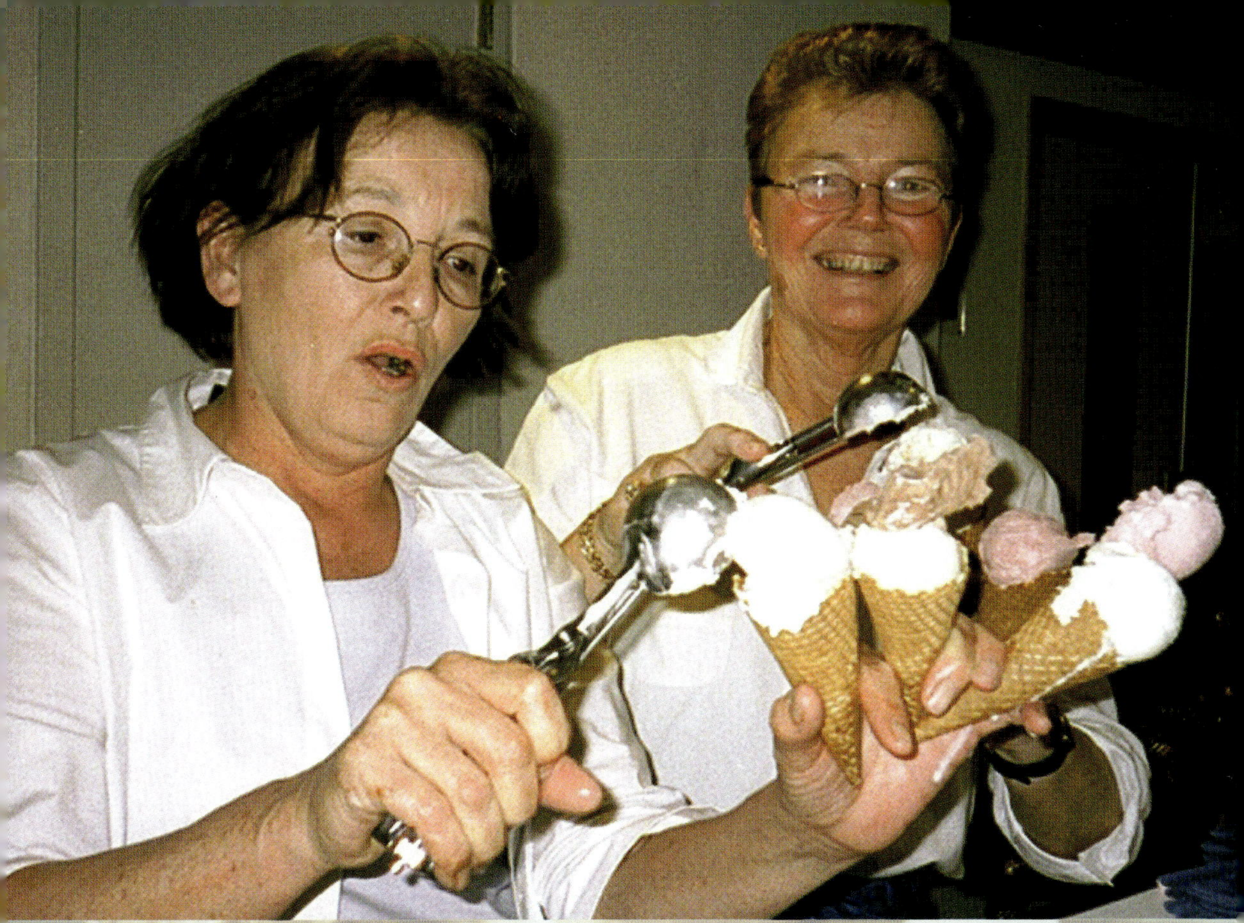

The ice-cone volunteer

story's mission statement. Especially in an organization like Humanitas, which attemps to guide the collective by their collectively disseminated core values, it might even lead to disruption.

A well-known variant of the idealist-volunteer, and clearly not often encountered at Humanitas, is the *religion-volunteer*, who might, in a different setting such as a confessional organization, prove to be the backbone of voluntary work.

Ad b. People seeking a social network or pastime are the second category of volunteer workers. The *recreational-, or pastime-volunteer*, who is just looking to spend his time pleasantly and fruitfully is most common. The many museum volunteer workers, putting themselves on the roll for fixed hours during the day, are an example of how their useful work may be combined with the pleasure of spending their time this way. It rather confirms the motto of the illustrious ancestors of squire Van Tets: "It is always important to have a suitable pastime in life, but take heed that it does not degenerate into actual work" and it also connects with the "use it or lose it" doctrine of Humanitas in general. A well-known sub-category of the above is the volunteer without a social network, who tries to compensate for the lack of social contacts. In this case the pastime alone is not satisfactory, unless there is interaction with others. It is another matter entirely for the *use it or lose it-volunteer* who is out of work and, while looking for another job, does not wish to lose the specific expertise of his occupation. Because such a person is dependent on maintaining his special skills, be it video films, or ICT-work, it is only prudent to find him the right work-allocation. At the reminiscence museum the clockmaker would fit the bill.

Ad c. Volunteer workers seeking psychological compensation are of the third category. The often encountered *bossy-volunteer*, with his compulsive need to dominate, is obviously more at home when placed with socially challenged youths, than with the feeble elderly, who are no match for him. A bossy-volunteer could be beneficial when groups of school children visit the museum, but it would certainly not be appropriate where elderly visitors are concerned. A special variant of the bossy-volunteer is the *nuisance-volunteer*, who has the neurotic habit of drawing attention to himself by being a nuisance. Such a person has often been thrown out of regular jobs before, and now wishes to have another go as a volunteer worker. He might be very energetic, knowledgeable and show dedication, but he may also be a disaster. Timely perception of the problem and addressing it, accompanied with some intervention on the part of the organization would in this instance be sorely needed supplements.

The *make-amends-volunteer* belongs to a special sub-category, and is often found in the care homes and institutions of Humanitas. A feeling of guilt for, for instance, neglect of care for deceased parents in the past, is being made up for in the present. The organization needs to be watchful that it is not exaggerated. Closely related to this, there is the volunteer worker who might be seen as a volunteer by persuasion because he, often at the advice of experts, is trying to re-join the labour process as a form of therapy. These *therapeutic-volunteers* who, with such attempt, are trying to build up a social network, and find a balance to their life's and working rhythm, are a very vulnerable group, and however beneficial they may be, will require much of the organization's attention and sometimes expert knowledge to deal with them. A sub-category of these volunteer workers could be called *boredom-volunteers*, who are bored at home and bored at work, and often find voluntary work boring as well, but finding the boredom of being bored just as boring, will try their hand at volunteer work. Knowing how to enthuse and inspire them and find purpose, qualities of such great value to the organization, will be an asset in these cases.

The so-called *psycho-volunteer* may be disastrous to have around. As they are often haunted by a psychical illness, such as kleptomania, themselves, it is adamant that the organization perceive the illness at an early stage, and decide whether something meaningful can still be realized with the available expertise and dedication, with the right assistance and support.

Ad d. A well-known category of volunteer workers are those who are looking for education or competence. Take, for instance, the *mono-volunteer*, who wishes to dedicate himself to one subject only, in order to become competent at it, such as with a special pastime, or having a mentally handicapped child, or a mother with aphasia, and therefore can only be employed for his specific subject-group. These volunteer workers may, during their stay, become absolute specialists on the subject and very valuable for those working in that particular field. The reminiscence museum has come across this category frequently. A sub-category of the mono-volunteer is the kind of volunteer worker also frequently known to Humanitas because of their multicultural approach, the so-called *naturalization-volunteer*, who wishes to learn through voluntary labour (an asylum seeker in the Netherlandsis forbidden to do paid labour) about the Dutch language and customs. The restorer / volunteer, channelling his general expertise to restore items for the museum, might also be called a mono-volunteer. The *network-volunteer* is looking to build an expertise-network in order to use this network, including the knowledge gathered over time, in his regular job. Obviously, this kind of volunteer needs to be offered the kind of voluntary work with a yield for his network, such as a management partnership. The *springboard-volunteer*, seeking to use his acquired network as a move up the ladder for a new position, which might cause him to end his voluntary work, may be a valuable addition, in the understanding that an allocation for long-term projects is, of course, out of the question.

Ad e. Humanitas distinguishes a rather special category of a very valuable and already frequently mentioned group of volunteer workers, with the wish to help either themselves, or their own group. These are the *client-volunteers*, the *partner-volunteers* and the *wrap-around care-volunteers*, often operating under more than one flag. Not only the dedication and expertise in general are of importance, but also the specific experiential knowledge focussed on one client only. To have this kind of particular expertise available is considered of the utmost importance to Humanitas, whereby the organization needs to act as a safety net, and take care that the volunteer work does not become too strenuous. A perfect example is found in the museum volunteer workers, focussing their attention particularly on the visitors with Alzheimer's.

Professional attention and government policy

The many different aspects encountered with volunteer workers and voluntary work may be an indication for the extent of professional attention required for voluntary labour. The organization ought to be aware of the pitfalls and take precautionary measures. For Humanitas, the most important guideline for volunteer work is the Humanitas extended-family approach, with co-optation as a recruitment factor.

Also extremely important is the measure in which the government policies can either contribute to, or break down the system. About the way volunteer work relates to regular labour, Willems will argue, that in this context there is every indication that the recent emphasis is put on regular labour participation, without involving volunteer work. Where not so long ago the inhumane and alienating aspects of (paid) labour were emphasised, nowadays the beneficial character of the official employment system is being preached, notwithstanding the rather lacking working conditions, and employment opportunities. Especially for those whose chances on rejoining the paid workforce are minimal, such as for the elderly unemployed, and the disabled, participation in voluntary labour could be an alternative.

The Humanitas Foundation wholeheartedly agrees with this and underlines the fact that it might even be a partial solution to the human resources problems in the elderly care. The government ought to be aware of this and either make a positive contribution or – at the least – prevent any negative effects of these government policies. There is no misunderstanding the clear reproof directed at the government, expressed by Willems, when he states that by continually emphasising the necessity for the best possible participation in the official employment system, the government is, in fact, instrumental in causing unpaid labour of all kinds, especially those of the caring or educational kind, to be rewarded an even lower social status than they already had.

Actually, the social status might be improved upon by the organizations themselves. At Humanitas one is admitted into the extended-family, volunteer-employment contracts are issued by the human resources department, and financial re-imbursements for volunteer workers are exploited to the limit. Dijkstal, writing an article "The grey revolution: hot, dynamic and sexy", mentions standing at the eve of one of the greatest social shifts in the composition of the European population: the grey revolution. Already one third of the Dutch population is over fifty, within twenty years half of the European population will be, in terms of marketing, considered "senior". He goes on to say that, nowadays, retirement is the beginning of a new phase in life, for some even the beginning of their true life. In this respect, the co-operation of the elderly in realizing a museum does offer a great variety of possibilities.

The average age of realistic activeness still on the increase, consequently increasing the potential time for doing voluntary work, provided it is important to the individual elderly person's life, might be advantageous to counterbalance the negative effects of a progressively ageing society. As Deth and Leijenaar express in their study, spending time on behalf of the organization will obviously also depend on a person's other existing activities. For people with a paid occupation, or with a house to keep, time allocation is different from, for instance, retired people.

Counterbalancing the progressively ageing society ought to be effectuated and facilitated. The volunteer worker should be offered what he, whilst realizing his own zest of life, is looking for. This can only be realized, if the organizations employing volunteer workers have expert knowledge of the different archetypes of volunteer workers and recognize the importance of coming up with the right mix. Often a specific allocation of tasks is necessary to avoid frustration and overburdening. Enjoyment, partnership, co-operation and mutual appreciation, all elements of the Humanitas extended family-approach, are as important.

Aside from this, good working conditions, such as a third party liability insurance, an expenses policy, the possibility to be promoted on account of expertise, "sharing the glory", are extremely important aspects when dealing with voluntary work, which goes for the museum as well.

De ja-cultuur als instrument voor humanisering van de zorg

Hans Marcel Becker

Summary of the Yes-culture

Living and working within the complexes of Humanitas are based on a new vision, which may be considered a guideline for the complete process of care and well-being. An important aspect of this care vision is what is by now known as "the yes-culture". The yes-culture presumes a "yes"; a "no" is NOT done. It goes so far as to actually exclude "no" to any idea or wish from clients, family, co-workers and volunteer workers, and "yes" to be the only appropriate response. This will stimulate residents and family to a great extent to come forth with wishes and ideas, be active, set up projects, and suggest changes. In essence: look positively at what is still within reach, instead of looking at what is not possible (anymore).
One could define the yes-culture as follows: "The yes-culture, by way of "saying no is forbidden", is a constructive and change-invoking way of management, and can be set off against a traditional control-culture, which is primarily focussed on continuity, and will ward off any unforeseen internal and external influences.
There are some interesting aspects from a managerial point of view: an improved business efficiency; an improved receptiveness toward the inner world of clients, wrap-around care, volunteer workers and employees; an improved open attitude toward the outside world; a strong promotion of creativity within all layers of the organization and the outside world; the yes-culture as atmosphere defining, and as politically strategic motivation; improvement of the image (being "more positive, and better") externally, as well as internally (the corporate identity); to facilitate negotiations; the impulse it provides for the "use it or lose it" approach, and last but not least the immediate financial implication (saying "no" will cost more money than you might think, on account of the loss of time and degenerating atmosphere).

In a yes-culture a large amount of time, and therefore money, is saved by reducing meetings to an absolute minimum, or even zero. Moreover, the time normally spent on updating rules and regulations and protocols is brought down as well. An expensive, sanctioning control system has also become superfluous.

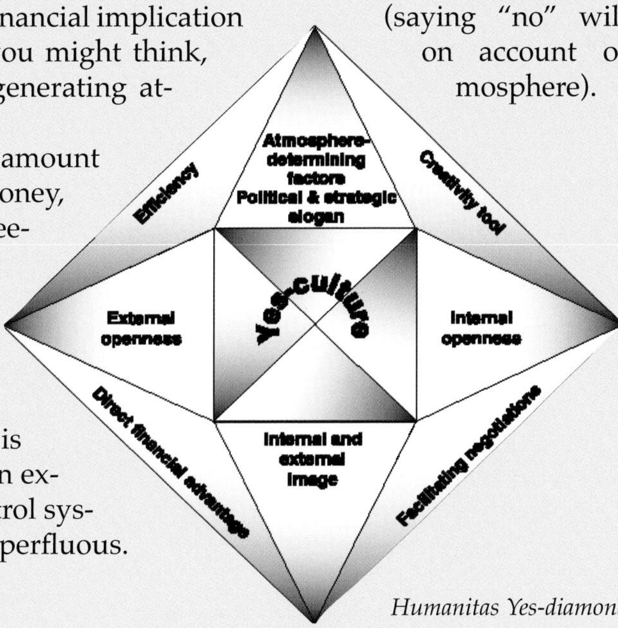

Humanitas Yes-diamond

Saying "yes" will stimulate the people on the work-floor, and the clients to be more creative and come up with ideas and plans. The open yes-culture enables the experiential expertise, assertiveness, and long-cherished, or spontaneous ideas of employees, clients, family and friends and the many volunteer workers, to be converted into improvements or innovations within the organization. This approach leads to a kind of co-partnership for everyone involved.

The resulting image of the "yes-culture" is one of : "at Humanitas anything is possible" and "it is different, better and more positive". This creates a positive image to the outside world and has a positive effect on the co-operation with stakeholders outside the organization.
Saying no always costs money, indirectly at any rate, as it is frustrating, creativity-killing , and creates absence through sick-leave. If saying no is accompanied by discussions and meetings, it will also become a direct money loss. Humanitas takes the view that every minute of a paid employee has a minimum price-tag of fifty euro cents. So, an hour's meeting with ten people will, not taking into account all the other disadvantages, represent a expense-item of €300. This means that a potential budget for a proposal may easily dwindle by discussing the pros and cons at length. Which means you have not accomplished anything, but have spent the money anyway.
Therefore, it is a better idea to start execution of the proposals on the table immediately, even if there is a chance of failure. An outsider might think that by saying yes to every query and wish, the success-rate for many plans must be slim. However, in practice only ten percent of the proposals are not feasible. But even in a stringent control-culture with its endless, monotonous, time and money consuming meetings, and budgeting one year in advance, many plans will not be feasible, maybe for those very reasons.
Actively applying the yes-culture will eventually lead to an ongoing flow of lively and problem-solving information about the clients' wishes. Besides, it will give employees a stimulus to report organizational problems, and come up with creative, constructive ideas to solve the problems there and then. A manager in the yes-culture is primarily some kind of film-director, with a creative, participating, inspiring and catalyst part. This kind of leadership involves acting on a vision, the corporate story, allowing partners as well as clients, suppliers as well as families, room to think and act coherently. In this way a corporate, continuously improved, overall vision will be developed, which will give guidance, processing experiences and ideas to give them substance and meaning.
As we argued earlier, the yes-culture is characterized by its open attitude towards residents, families, volunteer workers and employees. Their often long-standing experiential expertise and extensive knowledge of the daily

routine are an invaluable source of information upon which improvements are realized. Criticism and innovative ideas are, therefore, considered by Humanitas to be free advice, which merit to be rewarded with a happy "yes, that ought to be possible".
Contemporary emancipated clients and their families have every right to an explanation why things are done the way they are. They are curious about the possibilities and restrictions of the organization, and are certainly not prepared to be met with a crude and unexplained "no". Instead, they are asking to uphold the fundamental equality between clients, families, employees, volunteer workers, and yes, even management.
Which is why saying "yes" ought to be one of the core-attitudes for the employees at work. It goes without saying that everyone understands that not all things are feasible, if only because of the technical, or financial aspects. What one can do is start off with an initial "yes", and then approach the client and family with a humane, positive attitude, and start a dialogue to review the possibilities and find ways to come to a solution together. Please bear in mind that clients too, even when seriously handicapped, should fundamentally be able to be in control of their own lives. In doing so they should not be unduly restricted by the institutions. One of the aspects of the yes-culture is, that the Humanitas care organization assumes that only one person can decide what is good for him (as long as his brains are functioning) and that is the client himself. Even matters which are often not commonly condoned socially, such as having a shower once every three weeks, eating baked beans every day, keeping five cats, and getting drunk at the bar every day, would fit the bill. As everywhere else in society, the limits are set by the measure of inconvenience experienced by other people as a result of the client's wishes.

The yes-culture, therefore, extends far beyond the limits of politeness and receptivity. Clients and their social network are stimulated and actively supported by Humanitas in every way possible to remain in control of their activities ("use it or lose it") and by doing so, will be able to contribute best to the organization.
The "yes-culture" attitude is even expected to extend to the clients themselves, their partners and families, and volunteer workers as well. An attitude not yet familiar to many belonging to this social network, who are still regarding the institution as some kind of hotel. They, too, need to get used to the idea that matters they may not appreciate, but which are beneficial to the client, will be made possible. Children who live in fear of mother falling down will need to realize that their being paranoid is likely to be more dangerous than the falling itself. Hospitalization as a consequence of deliberate (overkill) care for the client, who himself still wishes, and is able (to some

extent), to be in control, may prove to be disastrous.
Fact is, that the yes-culture is instrumental in converting the experiences, active participation and long-cherished or spontaneous ideas of employees, clients, their families and the many kinds of volunteer workers, into improvements and (care) innovations. Those involved are active members of the Humanitas extended family, and all competences of this family are utilized to the full, by dialogue and active participation.
As shown by the above, the yes-culture, after true Humanist fashion, puts great trust in the independence, creativity and positive attitude of the whole organization, including their clients and families and volunteer workers. It might be regarded as the positive starting point of "yes".
Supervision, formal procedures and protocols etc. should certainly not dominate. An unusual occurrence in care-land in The Netherlands, with its jungle of ethical, moral, medical, paramedical, hygienic and industrial supervision rules.
As research results have shown, it is obvious that applying the yes-culture has significant advantages, and contributes considerably to the activation and wellbeing of all involved. Moreover, as a direct result from this, the living conditions are more agreeable than usually found in the care institutions.

Yes!
IDEA
WHISH

Corporate Stories

VERWOORDEN, VERTELLEN EN VERANKEREN

Astrid Schutte - Theo Hendriks

Kluwer
a Wolters Kluwer business

The Corporate Story of Humanitas

The corporate story of Humanitas; from "Corporate Stories": Humanitas – a practical example from the care sector.

The book "Corporate Stories" gives an in-depth analysis of the phenomenon of corporate stories and relates the corporate story of Humanitas, together with an elaborate analysis.

THE UPCOMING MOVEMENT OF A YES-CULTURE

The arrival of Hans Becker.
Hans Becker: "When I arrived here in 1992, the Humanitas organization was a hierarchy with 12 buildings, employing 1200 people and housing 1300 elderly. Everybody was walking around in a white coat and everything was managed via fixed protocols and instructions. An organization modelled on medical treatment, as were many similar organizations. If the organization was to be pictured as a pyramid, the doctors in their white coats would be at the top, and the clients and their families would be right at the bottom of the hierarchy. They were misery islands, as my father called them on hearing that I had accepted this job. In the nursing homes, the elderly were packed together in a ward, six at a time. The only privacy they had was a curtain which could be drawn around their beds. And of course everything was painted in white or grey, because that was considered "hygienic". Retching elderly were roaming the hallways. Visiting family kept their eyes on their watches to see how fast they could leave the premises with any decency. In the elderly homes things were not much better, they had small rooms of 20 square metres to live and sleep in.
Humanitas was also a very money-draining organization. It took a yearly loss of three million Dutch guilders, in the times before the euro. I am originally an economist by profession, and there is no doubt in my mind: a business run by professionals only, is expensive. The experiential expertise of clients and their family had not been taken into account. There was an atmosphere of: we are the ones taking care of the people. Consequently, there were many complaints. And that, too, cost a lot of money, about 50 eurocents per minute. Every complaint needed to be addressed, did it not? So, everything was expensive and rather unpleasant. Only after I had committed myself to the job, did I realize what I had let myself in for, so to speak. Oh yes, I had seen the splendid managing director's office during the interview, but not the rest. I thought: it is a fine salary, and it does not matter whether it is a hospital, or an office I'll be managing.

Make it fun!

In the beginning I did not have a corporate story at all. This developed over time. I just set out to make it more fun: redecorate the lobby and furnish it with murals and expositions. Allow for some chaos. It is a mess here, too, because the restaurant is open all day. Did you happen to see the antique wheel-chairs collection? You might call those examples of "conversation pieces" (something to talk about). When you are challenged in your abilities, as are most people around here, it is nice to have something to look at, and talk about. And you want to have a nice meal. Therefore, people can eat what they please, here. A dietician can be called upon to advice a client, if he wishes, but it does not mean she will look over his shoulder, or raise an admonishing finger. I am, with fifteen restaurants in our institutions, the largest restaurant owner in Rotterdam.

And the white coats needed to come off, as well. A flowered dress is just as hygienic as a white coat, is it not? As long as it is washed regularly.

Of course we have demolished those wards and have provided clients with bed-sit apartments, where they have privacy and their own belongings around them. Later on, I have introduced the "age-proof apartment" : two-bedroom apartments which are adaptable to the changing needs of clients, who are increasingly less mobile or require more care.

For the first years I have been improvising. Only after about seven years did I have a good look at what I had achieved, and how it had developed. Then I started to shape and formulate the ideas behind my intuition, and checked these ideas with scientific models. As a consequence of which I have taken my Ph. D. on a case-study of the changes I have accomplished here. At the moment I am a professor in "Humanization of Care" science, at the University of Humanistic Science in Utrecht, Holland. But that did not happen until 2005.

Human happiness

In 1992 I asked my management team: what do we consider to be our core-business? The response was: cure and care. But how realistic is curing and caring, when the clients who arrive here with their chronic handicaps will never get better? Statistically speaking, they will die within two-and-a-half years after admittance. And if we administer too much care, their deterioration will progress even faster. When you do not cook, or cleanse yourself anymore, after a while you will loose the ability to do so completely. Cure and care, I said, will only go so far. Let us start by having a closer look at the secondary aim, human happiness. Let us make that our core-business. At the same time it would enable me to make a beautiful connection to the Humanist way of thinking which is, ultimately, the starting point of the

Humanitas organization, where every human being is considered valuable within his own rights.
I may have side-tracked somewhat, but you need to realize that human happiness is very important. Over the last few years social psychology has increasingly focussed the attention on happiness and positive feelings, after years of exclusively discussing negative emotions. Aggression, depression .... such a diversity of problems, which needed to be solved. Positive people, however, appear to live longer, are happier, more creative, have more reserves to withstand the miseries of life, are more of a pillar of strength to their fellow men, or so they have discovered in social psychology. From the point of view of an economist, a positive attitude resulting in happiness, is therefore a very important factor.
Well, let us consider happiness. How did I go about making it more acceptable? Well, I am using external means to influence my employees. When I mention on TV, as happened recently on the National Healthcare Consulting hour (a Dutch television program) that happiness is our core-business, people think this is fantastic. But if I should mention this at one of our own New Year's receptions, people would be more sceptical: "Yeah, yeah, sure thing...".
We have film crews on site almost every month, all the broadcasting networks have been to visit us. We have been publicised in all the magazines. From professional magazines like "Healthcare and Business" to the leading Dutch newspapers. Which, by the way, is great for recruitment purposes. Up to this day there has not even been a need for external recruitment, new employees have approached us of their own accord. Everyone wants to be part of a success story, don't they? Which is what we are currently propagating when recruiting via our personnel.

Management by storying around

Fact is, that I am continually occupied with cultural steering. Cultural steering boils down to communication. The best way to do this is with stories and simple one-liners, which everyone will remember. I never stop telling stories, as you may have noticed. "Management by storying around" These one-liners I have come up with in practice, for instance "care with the hands at one's back" or "the mangy mongrel is just as important as any nurse". One-liners are easy to remember. You might say that they are the anchors to pin down a story with. Which is also the outcome of the research I have done on the subject.
Human happiness at an institution like this, is the result of four core values. Together, these four elements are the basis of our corporate story.

Self direction

Self direction is the first core value, as people need to decide for themselves how to live their lives. If they want to have a shower three times a day, that is fine. If they wish to bring their five cats along with them, it should be possible. I myself have a junkie for a foster son. He is now in his forties, has the looks of a twenty-eight year old, and has the mind of a twelve year old, after a lifelong habit of using dope, need I say more? Look, there he is. Comes to ask me for some money, I bet. Sometimes he is a nuisance, but most of the time he is a quite a distraction and he keeps the gossip alive.

Self empowerment

Self empowerment is another major core value. It is important to take care of yourself as much as possible. "Use it or lose it", is the slogan. Some time ago a lady said to me: "Mister Becker, I can put on my own support panty-hoses again!" It had taken her six months to regain the skill to do it, after years of having others doing the job for her. Using your own skills to get things done, that is what gives a person self-esteem. Therefore, one of the Humanitas one-liners is: do not take care of people, but take care that they take care of themselves and each other.

Extended family

The extended family is the third core-value. Because life here is not just about the client/patient, the family is also involved. When they like coming over for a visit, it will reflect on resident mother or father in a positive way. You need to give the family something interesting to talk about. Which is why we have so many paintings on the walls, and have a restaurant where they can all have a meal, and have set up the reminiscence museums. Some of the theme-rooms there have been designed as kitchens from the thirties, or fifties. There are children's rooms with toys from former days, and there is a shed with old tools. I shall take you over there myself, later.

Yes-culture as the driving force

The yes-culture, finally, is the driving force of the whole story. Saying "no" uses a lot of energy and is frustrating. It is a terrible waste, if only because you are for ever explaining why. The other day, for instance, a lady had screwed a screw-eye into the panel of her front-door. With a rope looped through it she was then able to slam the door shut from her wheelchair. "No", was the institution's first reaction, you cannot do such a thing with a brand-new door, can you? But I said: "Yes, we can! We are not in the business of unblemished doors! Everybody should have such a screw-eye in their door. Then they can attach a rope to it themselves if they need it". The yes-culture strengthens the weaker layers within the organization (clients, family, volunteer workers) and makes room for creativity and innovation. The four core-values have really not changed over time. What did change, however, is the effect it generates. In the beginning I, for one, had the idea that the partners of dementia residents would prefer to live with them. But it turned out that sometimes it was driving those partners mad. It is so frustrating when your partner's personality has changed so completely, as is often the case with dementia. I have also discovered the importance of a communal area. To have a designated place where everything happens around you, and where you can go for entertainment, like the atrium we have here, with a bar, a restaurant, supermarket, internet café, hairdresser's, etc. which gives the appearance of an indoor village square, is probably more important than having a spic and span apartment. And human beings are social animals, aren't they, and loneliness is the biggest handicap when you are elderly.

Dialogue.

The four core-values should not be seen as rigid protocols, but together form the basis for dialogue. That old lady who wanted to bring five cats with her was met with an initial "yes", after which we started negotiating with her. A "yes-culture" does not necessarily imply an unconditional "yes" to everything, as it is not always practical. The yes-culture should really be more of an attitude. And in her case it meant that we came up with the solution that she was to keep two cats herself, two cats were going to the lady next-door who had been obliged to dispose of her own cats, and one cat was to stay behind in her old home. When you say "yes" initially, and continue to negotiate, people are less inclined to complain at a later stage. Because they realize that we have gone out of our way to grant heir wishes. Another example concerns an elderly demented lady, who would go on a roaming spree once in a while. If it had been up to the Health Inspection, we would have had to restrain her, such as to tie her up, or confine the lady to a closed ward. But that seemed such an inhumane and unworthy solution. Especially because at times she still had her lucid moments. So, in consultation with her family, we decided not to do this. But three months later, on one of her roaming sprees, she fell in the canal and drowned. At first the family threatened to go to the health inspection, which, obviously, they were entitled to do. But we discussed the matter. "Should we have tied her up instead? " I asked. "Particularly as her bouts of confusion were only incidental?" Finally they realized that with a view to her well-being, this would not have worked out either.

The point of having a new culture with human happiness as its core business, is that you yourself must set the right example by saying "yes" as well. Which is the way we, the Board of Directors and management, are "relating" our corporate story. There are times that I have been known to get drunk at the bar here. I drink a bottle of Sancerre daily. Knowing full well that it is not good for my health, but I like it, anyway. Last year I married a Turkish boy of 31. Look, I'll show you our wedding photo. The point is: you and I want to be in control of our lives as well, don't we? The residents should, therefore, be able to do the same.

Resistance
Of course there is resistance. For instance in the past from the "College of Hospital Facilities". At the time it was a body of civil servants, consisting of so many little kingdoms of rules-and-regulations pushing officials. A large institutional kitchen had to be installed in the home for the elderly, nurses' stations and a special bath for the handicapped had become obligatory in the nursing home, even though we did not, in fact, need them. We then decided to contact the State Secretary of Health, who eventually concurred, after which matters changed for the better nationwide for the entire branch. An example of an obstacle on our path of a completely different calibre, concerns my unconventional approach for getting things done, and the image it creates. One day I made the papers with a story, of how I had popped 6.000 bottles of champagne in one year's time. There was an outcry "What a disgrace! To waste precious community funds on champagne, instead of using it to create more hands at the bedside!" I then had to explain, as an economist, how those bottles of champagne cost €3.95 a bottle. Half of them I give away for free. The other half I sell off in our bars and restaurants at €15.- per bottle. So macho son-in-law can buy mother a bottle as a present. The result is that in the end we get one whole care-nurse for free, and a lot of human happiness into the bargain: son-in-law happy, mother happy, daughter happy, and Humanitas happy as well. That is what I mean, though.
Relating the corporate story to guide the culture along the right path is an ongoing process. You do not stop the discussions, nor the dialogue. The story of Humanitas needs to be told at all levels. Studies have shown that everyone at Humanitas is familiar with the story and its essence will no doubt be passed on.

Pioneering
Over time the atmosphere of 1992 has changed completely, if only because we are doing much of the recruitment via our own personnel. Let me show you a copy of a flyer which I have distributed: the person who introduces a new employee, will receive €500. Which will guarantee you employment of similarly enthusiastic and active personnel. This way, the change has been brought about from the inside.

Am I a pioneer in the world of the elderly care? I believe I am. The yes-culture and the concept of age-proof housing, for instance, are real innovations and the reminiscence museums within these institutions might be considered innovative too.
Humanitas now owns 32 homes, has 2.200 employees, and about 4.000 elderly residents. I am now sixty five years of age, and have signed on for another three years. What will happen to the Humanitas story once I am gone? I wouldn't know. The problem lies in the fact that there are not really many people as crazy as I am. Fortunately, it is rather hard to "undo" a once established business culture. And the culture has changed completely. I did not do that all by myself. But I am indeed Chief Storyteller of the corporate story.

(Recorded by Astrid Schutte –www.storyventures)

The basic elements of a successful business story, which a corporate story will be judged upon by the authors.

The authors of Corporate Stories are looking at three aspects. At first, there is the "narrative" factor. Does the story have a heading, a narrative, and an ending? How was it before? What was the result? Who is the hero? What was the hitch? What brought about the change?

The "relating" factor is a continuance of the first. Is the story appealing? Will people be able to recognize themselves in it? Do they see themselves as part of the story? Finally, they look at the "anchoring" factor. Is the story visible? Does it express itself in every possible way, or is it tucked away in a drawer somewhere? And how did the story come into being? Is it someone's personal story or does it really relate to the whole organization?

The story needs to have some measure of truth. But should it necessarily be true? Yes and no: on the one hand, it should not be untrue. On the other, there is no need for it to be absolutely true, but either way the story needs to be accurate. The art lies in framing the story in the right manner. How does the story get shaped? Which characteristics, values, and events are being accentuated? In which context? Whom is the story designated for and whose involvement is required? If this is done well, the corporate story will become a forceful instrument: outstanding, engaging and indicative.

ANALYSIS BY THE AUTHORS OF THE CORPORATE STORY OF HUMANITAS

Humanitas: A story of revolution.
Managing director of Humanitas, Hans Becker, on his arrival in 1992, began to alter the management structure. Parallel to this alteration, Becker started to promote his vision, inside as well as outside the organization, of the much needed revolution; management by storying around. Thus began the corporate story of Humanitas, which has since been told in ever varying ways. The story scores highly on all three factors.

Narrative factor: the Humanitas-story has a clearly identifiable hero: Hans Becker, who needs to overcome obstacles to reach his goal and who meets adversaries (for instance the "College of Hospital Social Securities") and helpers (co-workers) along the way. The Humanitas-story about the yes-culture is pre-eminently the story of Hans Becker. The corporate story has, therefore, been set up as a monologue, and one where the reader is addressed very directly. It is rather interesting that Becker does not fall into the trap of describing himself as being perfect, like some novel-character, who is a Mr. Perfect, and therefore too dull to be interesting. Becker has shown courage in giving himself a dose of rebel-characteristics, which only serve to enhance the credibility of the story. And the real leading actors, the clients, family members, and volunteer workers are well and clearly portrayed.

Relating factor: The Humanitas-story is very concrete. The obstacles Becker has encountered, as well as the ultimate goal (the yes-culture), are being illustrated with examples. In those examples people always play an important part, managers, co-workers and residents alike. All their perspectives are given equal opportunities, which helps in passing the story on. Becker clearly demonstrates the resistance against him, which makes him more convincing as a leader. One of the most remarkable signs that the Humanitas-story scores highly on the relating scale, is the continual attention from the media for the Humanitas-practice and its ideas.

Anchoring factor: The fact that Hans Becker is undoubtedly the most important hero and storyteller of the Humanitas-story, is unmistakable proof of his commitment. He never stops propagating, in various ways, the corporate story of Humanitas. His ideas and slogans about the yes-culture are known even outside the organization. The commitment of the Humanitas employees to the story is shown exclusively by the number of innovations Becker has implemented, which would not have seen the light of day without them. Becker does not only speak about "I", but often about "we", accentuating the together-ness of the Humanitas employees. Without them the story of the yes-culture would not have been possible. Finally, the Humanitas-story is being told consistently (communication), for the most part by word of mouth, and usually with the aid of external storytellers (journalists).

THE CORPORATE STORY CARRÉ OF HUMANITAS

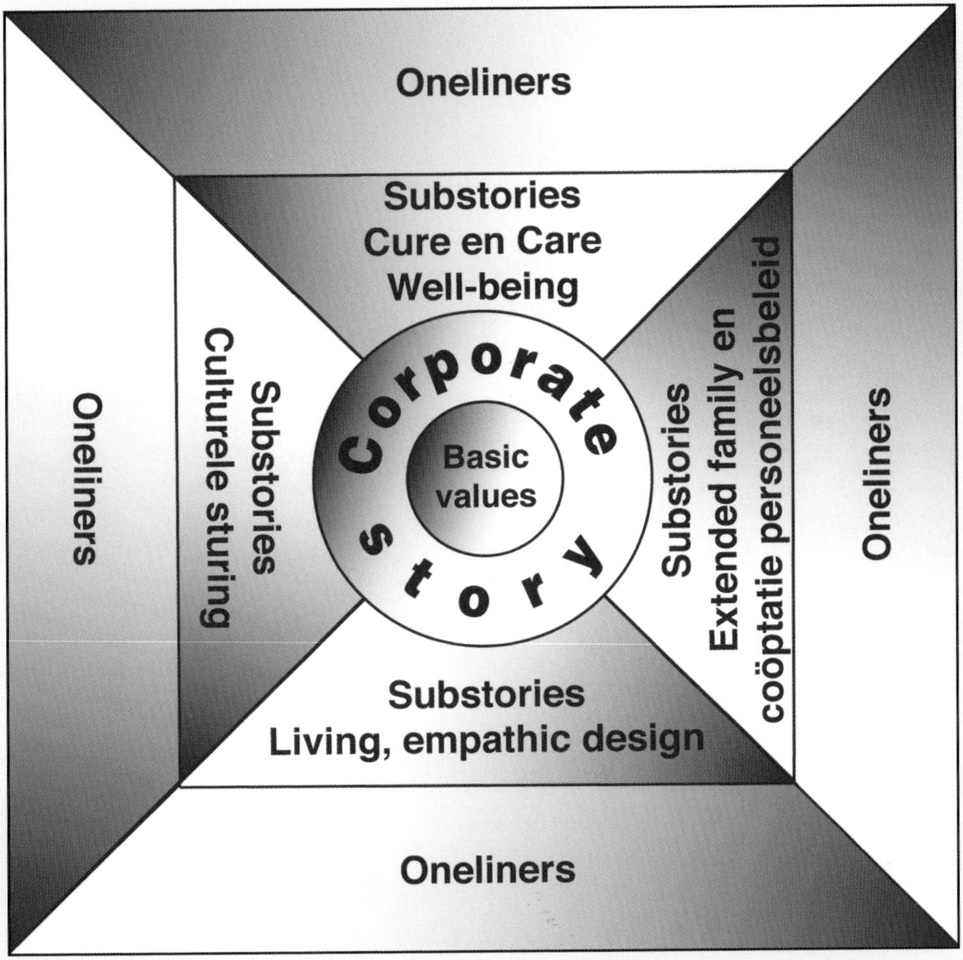

Bibliography

Anderson, G. *Reinventing the museum,* Historical and Contemporary Perspectives on the Paradigm Shift, Lanham, Maryland 2004

Becker, H.M. *Het herinneringsmuseum als instrument bij de humanisering van de ouderenzorg:* "Van misère-eiland naar tempel van cultuur" Humanitas, Rotterdam 2008

Becker, H.M. *Levenskunst op Leeftijd,* Eburon, Delft 2003

Becker, H.M. *De ja-cultuur als instrument voor humanisering van de zorg,* Humanistic University Press, Utrecht 2006

Bender, M., Banckham, P. & Norris, A. *The therapeutic purposes of reminiscence,* Safe Publications, London 1999

Bendien, E.M., From the Art of Remembering to the Craft of Ageing, A Study of the Reminisence Museum at Humanitas, Rotterdam

Benoit, L. *Musées et muséologie,* Presses Universitaires de France, Paris 1970

Bos, R. ten *Kwaliteit in bedrijf,* 'We hebben spookrijders nodig in onze organisatie' 19e jrg. nr. 3, Amsterdam april 2003

Draaisma, D. *Waarom het leven sneller gaat als je ouder wordt,* Rainbow Paperback, Amsterdam 2003

Engelen, J. NIZW en Civiq, *Vergrijzing of verzilvering.* De effecten van vergrijzing op vrijwilligerswerk, maart 2004

Fonville, E. *Het verleden in het Heden, het reminiscentiemuseum van Humanitas,* Afstudeerscriptie EUR, Rotterdam 2006

Gezondheidsraad *Omstreden herinneringen,* Den Haag 2004

Gigerenzer, S. *De kracht van je intuïtie,* Kosmos, Antwerpen 2007

Halbwachs, M. *On collective memory,* University of Chicago Press, Chicago, Illinois 1992

International Council of Museums *ICOM Code of Ethics for Museums,* London 2006

Katriel, T. *Performing the Past.* A study of Israeli Settlement Museums, Lawrence Erlbaum Ass., Mahwah, New Jersey 1997

Kemp, M. *Reminiscence aids,* Department of Health and Social Security, London 1979

Meeus, T-J. *Oma traint haar brein,* NRC Handelsblad zomerbijlage, 2007

Moscoviter, H. *Open de luiken van uw geheugen,* Stichting Humanitas en Hofnar Producties, Rotterdam 2006

Nora, P. *Between memory and history: Les Lieux de mémoire,* Representations 26, Spring: 7-24. 1989

Neal, A. *Help for the small museum,* Pruett Publishing, Boulder, Colorado 1969

Parnassia Project Depressies bij Ouderen, Parnassia Den Haag 1998

Puyenbroeck, J. van *Reminiscence in ageing people with intellectual disabilities,* Katholieke Universiteit, Leuven 2006

Sandell, R. *Social inclusion, the museum and the dynamics of sectoral change,* Museum and Society 1, 1: 45-62, University of Leicester 2003

Sanders, K. *Herinneringsmuseum,* Haagse Hogeschool, Den Haag 2007

Scherpen, J. *Invloed van Social Sharing op de cognitieve en sociale integratie van emotionele gebeurtenissen meegemaakt tijdens oorlogs- of crisissituaties,* Open Universiteit Nederland, Heerlen 2001

Schutte, A. & Hendriks, Th. *Corporate Stories verwoorden, vertellen en verankeren,* Kluwer, Amsterdam 2007

Staatsuitgeverij *Verkennend onderzoek naar musea in Nederland,* Den Haag 1972

Unesco Press *The organization of museums, practical advice,* Paris 1978

Unruh, D. *Toward a Social Psychology or reminiscence,* in: Unruh, D. and Livings, G.S. Current Perspectives on Ageing and the Life Cycle, JAI Press inc, London 1989

Biography Professor dr. Hans Marcel Becker

Hans Becker was born during World War II on Februari 16, 1942 in Rotterdam's bombed inner city. In this city he obtained his Master's degree in Economic Sciences at the Erasmus University. In 1969 he was installed at his Alma Mater as assistant professor 'institutional economics and history of economic thougt'

In 1984 he was invited to accept the position of Managing Director for the Humanitas Association, focussed on elderly care and social work. Thus, he combined giving lectures with his management activities at Humanitas.

In 1992 he was singled out by a head hunter bureau for the position of Chairman of the Managing Board of the Humanitas Foundation, with 3500 employees and a turn-over of 135 million euro.
He 'fathered' the concept of age-proof living and the Humanitas philosophy.

Aside from this fulltime job, Hans Becker has been (and still is) active as chairman in a variety of foundations, boards and consultancies, among which a renowned high tech company and world-famous archtitectural company. Hans Becker is Honorairy Consul of the Republic of Mali in the Netherlands.

In 2003 Hans Becker received his Ph.D. at the University of Humanistic Sciences, Utrecht. This was followed in 2005 by this inauguration as Extraordinary Professor of 'Humanization of Care' at this university. Hans Becker has also been an instructor at the Office of Executive Education Harvard University U.S.

In 2010, at the age of 68, Hans Becker withdrew as Chairman of the Board and accepted the function of Ambassador in active service for the Humanitas Foundation. He now dedicates his energy and creativity to further the cause of Humanitas and safeguarding the Humanitas philosophy in all its aspects.

Mr. Becker was awarded the Erasmus medal and the Van Borsselen medal by the City of Rotterdam and the 'Erasmus on Horseback' medal by the Erasmus University, and was presented the Cape Verdean-Dutch friendship medal by the Ambassador of the Republic of Cape Verde.
In January 1997 Her Majesty the Queen of The Netherlands appointed Mr. Becker Officer in the Order of Oranje Nassau, a knighthood of the Queen.
Mr. Becker received the Zorgvisie (care vision) Excellence Trophy with the associated title: National Care Manager of the Year. In 2006 he received the highest decoration of the province of South-Holland, the Golden Lily. Mr. Becker published several books and articles in the field of history of economic thougt and in the field of humanising the care sector.

A reminiscence museum seems easy to construct but it is much "blood, sweat and tears" and more transpiration than inspiration.
The result is brilliant.
Do give it a try!